Little Threads: Or, Tangle Thread, Silver Thread and Golden Thread, by the Author of 'little Susy'.

Elizabeth Prentiss

And then she and Golden Thread went all about the farm.—P. 140.

LITTLE THREADS;

OR,

TANGLE THREAD, SILVER THREAD, AND GOLDEN THREAD.

BY THE AUTHOR OF "LITTLE SUSY."

With Illustrations by Absolon.

LONDON:

JAMES NISBET AND CO., 21, BERNERS STREET.

———

1864.

LONDON:

PRINTED BY EDMUND EVANS,

RAQUET COURT, FLEET STREET.

LITTLE THREADS.

CHAPTER I.

HERE was once a very beautiful piece of white satin, which had been woven with care and skill. Yet those who saw it went away shaking their heads, saying: "What a pity! what a pity!" For there ran across this lovely fabric a tangled thread; and that one thread spoiled all.

And there was a lady who was very beautiful, too. She had always lived in a pleasant home, with kind and loving friends about her. She had never in her life known what it was to want anything she could not have. Indeed, she seemed born to be treated gently and tenderly. People who were ignorant were not afraid to go to see and talk with her, for they knew she never laughed at their mistakes; and poor people liked to go and tell her about their poverty, just as if she were poor, too. And those who were sick or in trouble wanted her to know all about their trials. For those who went to see her with empty hands, came away not half so poor as they went in; and the sick and the sorrowful were comforted by her words of pity.

You will think that this lady who was so good, who could dress just as she pleased and ride when and where she pleased—who had friends to love her and friends to admire her—must have been very happy indeed. And so she was, for a time. Her life looked as smooth and fair as the white satin you have just heard of. But by and by there began to run across it a thread not at all like the soft and even threads of which it was made: here came a soiled spot—there were knots and tangles; as far as you could see, its beauty was gone. How did this happen? Why, there came into the house one day a little baby—a little, soft, tender baby, that did not look as if it would harm anybody. Its mother was very glad to see it. She thought herself almost too happy with such a treasure. The most sunshiny, pleasant room in the house was given this little thing for its own. All sorts of pure white garments were bought for it, and everything possible was done to keep it well and make it happy. Before it came, its mother used to lie down to sleep at night as sweetly as you do, little rosy child, who read this book. But now she slept, as people say, with one eye and one ear open. That is, she kept starting up to see if it were nicely covered with its soft blankets, or to listen to its gentle breathing, to know if it were quite well. If it happened to be restless or unwell, she would sit up all night to take care of it, or walk with it hour after hour, when anybody but its own dear mother would have been out of patience, or too tired to keep awake.

And before the baby came there, this lady used to spend a good deal of time at her piano, singing and playing. She used to draw and paint, and read and write. But now she almost forgot she had any piano. The baby's cooing was all the music she cared for. And she left off drawing and painting, and thought the sweetest picture in the world was that tiny, sleeping creature in its cradle. To be sure, mother and baby together did make a very lovely picture indeed. As for books, she had not now much time to read anything but *Combe on Infancy*, which she studied every day, because it is a book about babies, and tells how to wash and dress them, and what to give them to eat.

Perhaps you will begin to think that this lady loved her baby too much. But no; a mother cannot do that, unless she loves it better than God, and this little child's mother loved God best. She loved Him so dearly, that if He had asked her to give it back to Him, she would have given it without a word; He would not ask her to do it without tears.

CHAPTER II.

THE baby had a name of its own, but it was called "THE BABY," and nothing else, just as if there never had been one in the world before, and never would be again. As it had nothing to do but to grow, it did grow, but not very fast. Its mother said she liked a tiny baby better than she did a big one. When she showed it to her friends, she always said: "It isn't a very large child, I know; but you see its bones are very small, and of course that makes a difference." And they would reply: "Certainly, that makes a great difference. And it has the prettiest little round face, and wee bits of hands and feet, there ever were!"

The day on which the nurse who took care of the baby and its mother at first, was obliged to go away, another young woman came to fill her place. Her name was Ruth. She was very glad to come, indeed. For she thought it would be very nice to sit in that bright, pleasant room, holding that pretty little baby on her lap. She thought she should never know a care or a trouble. But she was quite frightened when she undertook to wash and dress the pretty little creature, to find how it screamed. The truth is, if there was any one thing this baby could not bear, it was to be touched with water. What was to be done? Let it go unwashed? Oh, no! that would never do! Its mother really trembled when she saw such a young, feeble creature cry so. She knelt down by the side of the nurse, and with her soft hands tried to hurry through the washing and dressing. They never knew how they got on the little shirt, or how they fastened on the little petticoats, or which of them tied the clean white frock. The nurse was red and warm, and the mother pale and tired, when this great task was over. But they both thought things would go better next time; and Ruth said so to herself as she walked up and down trying to quiet the child, and the mother said so to herself as she lay all worn out on the sofa, watching them.

Day after day passed, however, and every morning the baby screamed. As it grew older and stronger, its mother was less frightened when it cried; but it was painful to hear such an uproar, and she began to dread the hour for washing and dressing it.

" What can be the reason the baby cries so ?" she asked the nurse every morning; till at last, tired of saying,

" Perhaps she won't cry so next time," poor Ruth cried out,

" Why, it's the temper, ma'am !"

" Its temper!" said its mother, much astonished. " Why, I should as soon think of talking about the temper of one of the cows in your father's farm-yard !"

" And you might well do that, ma'am ; for cows has tempers of their own as well as babies and other folks. There was old White Spot, now. She couldn't cry and scream like this baby, but she could kick over a pail of milk equal to anybody, and did it many a time when she was put out."

The baby's mother hardly knew what to think. *Combe on Infancy* did not say a word on this subject. She thought she would write to her own mother, who lived not far off, and beg her to tell her whether little babies really did cry because they were angry, and ask her advice about a great many other things just as important. There was a small spot on the child's forehead, and she wanted to know if that would be likely to go away of itself. And how soon would the baby begin to "take notice ?" And what playthings had she better be buying, to be ready for it when it was ready for them? And, oh! how would it do to tie up a raisin in a rag, and stop the baby's mouth with that while they were washing it? For Ruth said she was sure that would do so nicely!

CHAPTER III.

THE baby grew older and grew stronger, but it did not grow better. The truth is, it had a very strong will of its own. As long as it could have its own way, it was pleasant and sweet; but the moment other people undertook to have their way, it began to scream.

As soon as it became old enough to understand what was said to it, and that was very soon, its mother resolved never to give it things for which it cried. She told Ruth so. But one day she went into the nursery, and there lay Miss Baby fast asleep on the bed, with a china vase on each arm.

" Why, Ruth, what does this mean?" she asked.

" The baby cried so for the vases that I could do nothing with her," replied Ruth. " It was time for her nap, and I did all I could to get her to sleep, but she cried herself nearly into fits for the vases. So at last I had to give them to her. She dropped right off to sleep then, like a lamb."

"Never do so again, Ruth. You may spare yourself a little trouble for the time, by giving a child what it cries for. But in the end you increase your trouble tenfold, and strengthen the child in its resolution to have its own way."

When the baby awoke, it did not miss the vases, which its mother had replaced on the shelf; but when it was ready to go to bed that night, it looked at them, and stretched out its arms towards them, saying plainly by its gestures: " I am going to sleep with those pretty things in my arms."

"No, baby can't have them," said Ruth. "Baby must go to sleep."

Baby's answer was a fearful scream, which was heard in the dining-room where her papa and mamma were taking tea.

"Hark!" said her papa. "I hear the baby. She has either had a fall, or there are a dozen pins pricking her."

"No, that is not a cry of pain," replied her mother. "It is a cry of anger. And I think I know what it means. However, I'll go up and see."

She ran up stairs, and found poor Ruth walking up and down with the child, looking hot and tired.

"I knew you would think I was murdering her,

ma'am," she said. "But it's those vases she wants. Wouldn't it be best to pacify her with them? She's hoarse with crying."

"No, Ruth, no," said her mamma. "I do not wonder you are tired and almost discouraged. But we must think of the child's good rather than our own present comfort."

She took the angry baby in her arms, and sat down sadly in a low chair with it.

"You are sure there are no pins about its clothes?"

"Oh! yes, ma'am! I sewed on its clothes just as you bid me."

"Very well. Go down now to your tea."

"I don't like to leave you with the child crying so."

"I prefer you should go. She will certainly stop crying before long."

Ruth went slowly down stairs.

"Two sticks an't crosser than that baby," she said to herself. "I never saw such a child. Why, every bone in me aches like the toothache."

"What's going on up stairs?" asked the cook, as Ruth entered the kitchen.

"You might knock me down with a straw," replied Ruth. "I have been trying for an hour to get the baby to sleep, and it has screamed the whole time, till I was afraid it would kill itself."

Meanwhile the poor mother still sat sadly and quietly in the low chair, holding the struggling child, and praying to God to teach her how to subdue it. She begged Him to give her patience, and to give her gentleness, and to give her firmness. The baby's cries began to grow less and less noisy, and at last, all tired out, it fell asleep. Its mother looked down upon it tenderly, and kissed it over and over. But her heart was full of care and pain.

"Ah!" thought she, "the old saying is true. Every rose has its thorn!"

CHAPTER IV.

DAY after day passed on, and the baby grew from a baby into a little child with busy hands, and active feet, and a will of its own that seemed to grow with its growth and strengthen with its strength.. Her father, seeing how much anxiety and trouble she caused her mother, began to call her "Tangle Thread," instead of "baby." By degrees, everybody in the house fell into the same habit, and instead of bearing her own sweet name of "Lily," this new name was fastened to her.

When she was two years old she could talk quite plainly, and when nothing was vexing her, she was bright and playful. Her mother tried to avoid conflicts with her as much as possible. But if she once began, she did not yield. She knew that no child can be happy that always has its own way. She knew that God would be displeased with her if she let her little daughter grow up self-willed and disobedient.

Early one morning, Tangle Thread awoke, smiling and cheerful. Her little crib was close by her mamma's bed, and she saw that neither her father nor mother was yet awake. She sat up in bed and played awhile with her pillow. But she was soon tired of that, so she climbed from her crib to the bed, and from the bed slipped down to the floor. Pretty soon her mother, hearing a slight noise, awoke, and starting up, she saw Tangle Thread standing in a chair before her father's dressing-table, with a razor open in her hand.

"Oh! she has a razor!" she said, jumping from the bed, and hastening towards the child.

Tangle Thread instantly got down from the chair, and ran across the room with the razor in her hand.

"Tangle Thread, stop this instant!" cried her father, awakened by the noise. But Tangle Thread only ran faster; and when she saw her father and mother both running after her, she became angry.

"*Will* have it! *will* shave!" she cried.

"Stop this instant!" cried her father once more.

By this time her mother had seized her hand, and after a struggle, the razor was secured. Tangle Thread burst into frantic screams, but suddenly stopped short when she saw that her mother's hand was covered with blood.

" Yes, you made your poor mamma cut her hand," said her father.

Tangle Thread was frightened.

" I sorry," she said.

But in an instant she was angry with herself for being sorry. She began to dance up and down, and to scream out: " No, no, not sorry."

Her mother was used to such scenes. Her father had never seen her so angry.

" Why, this is dreadful!" he cried. " I never saw such a child. If she does not learn to obey, she will some time cut herself to pieces or get burned up."

" Yes, I know it," replied her mother. " I have tried in every possible way to teach her obedience; but nothing seems to have any effect. Not half an hour after being punished for this offence, she will do something else just as bad."

" But has the child no feeling? It seems so unnatural for a little thing of her age not to be alarmed and pained at the sight of blood. And your fingers are all cut, I do believe. Let me see. Yes, every one of your poor mamma's fingers is cut and is bleeding," he said, turning to Tangle Thread, who during this time had not ceased to scream and stamp with all her might. Her father's address only made her cry more angrily and loudly.

C

Her mamma said to him in a low voice: " Do not notice her.   It only irritates her yet more. She has a great deal of feeling, and I am sure she is distressed at the sight of my cut fingers."

And this was true. Tangle Thread was distressed.   But she did not know herself what was the matter with her, and she was still angry and excited and kept on crying.   And when she once begun to cry, she was like a horse that has begun to run, and the more he runs the more he must run, till he gets almost wild and quite worn out, and has to stop to take breath.

CHAPTER V.

WHEN Tangle Thread had cried till she could cry no longer, her mamma sent for Ruth to come and dress her.

During breakfast, the father and mother were both silent and thoughtful. At last her father said:

" Do not you intend to bring that child to her senses, my dear?"

" Yes; I shall punish her by and by. Now, while she is so excited, she would let me kill her before she would give up."

" But you intend to make her say she is sorry?"

" I don't know."

" You don't know, my dear? Do you mean that you do not intend to break that child's will?"

" I used to think I must do that, once for all," she replied. " I have heard great stories of conflicts between parents and children, that finished up the business for ever. There's Mr. Hamilton; he told me that his little Ellen, when she was about a year and a half old, was standing near him, holding a little doll in her hand.

" 'Let papa see your dolly,' said he.

" The child put both her hands behind her, and made no answer.

" 'Come to me, and let me see your dolly,' he repeated.

" The child refused. At last, after urging her some time, he said :

" 'Then papa will have to make you do it.' He began by slapping her hands. She changed the doll from hand to hand, but held it firmly. He then used a little rod. The child grew more and more violent ; a regular battle raged between them. He kept repeating, 'I shall punish you, Nelly, till you show me your dolly ;' but she would not yield. At last she threw it at him, angrily. Hour after hour passed, before the child would submit; but at last she gave up, and that was their final conflict. But I have had twenty such scenes with Tangle Thread. She yields at last, and is as sweet and gentle and loving, for a time, as need be. But perhaps the very next day the whole ground will have to be fought over again."

" Perhaps Tangle Thread would yield to me

more readily," said her father. "As it was my razor about which she was so obstinate, perhaps I ought to take her in hand myself."

So, after breakfast, he took Tangle Thread into his dressing-room, and said to her:

"You have been a very naughty child; you would not mind either papa or mamma; and you made poor mamma cut her fingers very badly. Are not you sorry you were so naughty?"

Tangle Thread held down her head, and was silent.

"Answer papa. Are you sorry?"

No answer.

He took her little hand in his. "I shall slap this little hand very hard, if you do not answer me."

Then Tangle Thread burst out into her usual scream.

Her father struck her hands again and again, but she only kept on crying.

He began to wish he had not undertaken the task of conquering such a child.

"After all, it is a mother's work," he said to himself. He looked at his watch. "It is ten o'clock. I ought to be in my office," he said, uneasily.

"Tangle Thread, are you going to obey me, or shall I have to punish you more severely?"

Ten minutes passed—fifteen—Tangle Thread had no thought of yielding.

At eleven o'clock her father sat in despair, looking more worn out than the angry child did; but the battle was not yet ended.

At last her poor mother, who had sat looking on in agony, burst into tears.

"O my child!" she cried, "will you make your father strike you yet more!"

Then Tangle Thread's stubborn heart seemed to melt. She cried out:

"*Am* sorry, papa!"

"Then run to your dear mamma, and tell her so."

Tangle Thread ran into her mamma's arms, who kissed her and wept over her, but was too tired and heart-sick to say much.

Do you know, my little child, that your mamma feels just so when you are naughty, and have to be punished? She certainly does. Then won't you try to be good for her sake?

CHAPTER VI.

TANGLE THREAD fell asleep in her mamma's arms. Her papa looked at her sorrowfully.

"I am sorry I undertook to govern her," said he. "I never was so tired in my life. Who would think that that tiny frame could hold such a will!"

"I never have these conflicts with her now," replied her mamma. "It has been suggested to me, that when a child refuses to obey, it is best to punish it for disobedience at once, rather than enter on a contest with it. And, on the whole, I believe it to be the proper way."

"Well, good-by, my dear; it is past twelve, and I ought not to stay another moment. Do go and lie down. You look quite worn out. Or shall I order the carriage for you! Ah! your life is very different now from what it used to be before this strange child dropped down upon us!"

"It may look hard to those who only see the

wilful, wayward ways of the child," said her mother. "But I love this poor little creature dearly."

The father now kissed the pale mother and the sleeping child, and went out. He soon forgot, in trying to make up for his lost time, what he had been through. God means that the work of training little children should belong chiefly to the mother. She has no business to call her out; she can have no business so important outside her own doors. It is for her to watch every look and word and tone, to give up all her time, if necessary, and find her happiness in seeing her child grow up good and gentle, or her sorrow in seeing it continue perverse and disobedient. So Tangle Thread's mamma could not go out, like her papa, and forget her troubles. There was only one place in all the world where she could find comfort. That was on her knees, before God. She placed the weary little sleeper on her own bed, and then, with many tears, gave her away more truly than ever before to Him. She told Him all her troubles and cares, and besought Him to look down in love on her poor little lamb, and to take her in His arms, and carry her in His bosom, till she should become like Himself.

Perhaps you think that God heard this prayer and answered it at once, so that Tangle Thread awoke from her nap quite another child, and never was naughty again. And no doubt He did hear and answer it. But fruit does not ripen in one day, nor in two. Under the care of the skilful gardener it will surely ripen, but it must have sun and rain, not once or twice, but day after day, week after week—sometimes, even, month after month.

Poor little Tangle Thread was only conquered for a time. The very day after the sad affair with the razor, she was as naughty as ever. And the next day it was just the same. No matter what she was refused, she always cried for it with her whole heart. No matter how she was punished, she would do, right over again, the very things she had been forbidden.

Ruth found it hard work to get on with her; for when her mamma was out, she could cry as much as she pleased, and tease Ruth till her patience was worn, as she said herself, " to tatters."

" If you won't scream once to-morrow," Ruth said to her one day, " I'll ask your mamma to let you go home with me some time. Then you can see all our cows, and our hens and chickens, and you can take a basket and hunt for eggs."

" Well!" said Tangle Thread.

But the next day she cried half-a-dozen times. Once it was because her hair was cut; once because she did not wish to go to walk. Again, because there was rice-pudding for her dinner, and she said she hated rice; and so on, through the day.

"Try again to-morrow," urged Ruth.

"Well!" said Tangle Thread, "if you'll promise not to wash my face, nor change my dress, nor make me wear overshoes when I go out; if you'll go on the shady side of the street, and walk down to Union Square, then I won't cry. I shan't have anything to cry about."

"But I can't promise," said Ruth.. "I *must* wash your face and change your dress; I must put on your overshoes; and while this cold weather lasts, I must walk on the sunny side of the street. Your mamma has bidden me to do all these things; and as for Union Square, you know your mamma won't let you go there, because she is afraid you'll get run over."

"Then I shall cry," returned Tangle Thread. "Of course, if you and mamma do all you can to plague me, and won't let me do a thing I want to do, I *must* cry. Or, at any rate, I must fret."

"You think if we let you alone, and you could do just as you pleased, you would have nothing to cry or fret about. But you'd go to destruction in the space of half-an-hour. You would kill yourself eating cake and candy, or you would get run over by some cart or carriage, or you would catch your death of cold. It frightens me to think what you would do, if it wasn't for your poor mamma slaving herself into a consumption to make you a better child. And your mamma is such a sweet lady, too. Oh! I wish you would be a good child!"

But Tangle Thread was much amused at the various ways in which Ruth said she might go to destruction; and she liked better to hear that sort of talk than talk about being good, which was quite an old story.

"Tell some more dreadful things I might do," said she.

"I've told enough," said Ruth.

"You *must* tell me some more. Mamma says you must do all you can to amuse me. Come, make haste! Suggest something else!"

"Well, you might get choked to death trying to say a big word."

"Now you are laughing at me. And I've a right to say ' suggest' if I've a mind. I'll tell mamma how you laugh at me!"

Ruth answered good-naturedly: " I didn't mean to tease you, at any rate. Come, let me tell you all about my father's farm."

"You're always telling that. You've told me nine hundred times. I'd rather hear about something else."

" Then I'll tell you about the Babes in the Wood."

"No, I don't want to hear that, either. Tell me about a nurse that put a baby in a carriage, and made a poor little lamb draw it all over town. And at last the poor little lamb fell down dead."

"But I don't know that story."

"Yes, you do; for I've just told it to you."

"But if I only tell just what you've told me, you will get angry and go to crying."

"I told you all I know," said Tangle Thread. "I made it up myself. And you must tell me a lot more about it."

"But I can't," said Ruth. "I can't make up stories. I never could."

"You're a naughty girl. I don't like you one bit. I'll tell mamma of you."

"And you are a tiresome, naughty child," Ruth was tempted to say. But she bit her lips, and was silent. Then Tangle Thread ran away behind the bed, and was silent too. Ruth knew she would sit there and pout a long time, and then, if not noticed, scream till attention was paid her. She got up and opened her bureau-drawer, and took from it three little bits of candy.

"Here is some candy your mamma said I might give you," said she. "Come, get up from the floor and eat it."

Tangle Thread remained lying flat on the floor, with her face hidden in her two hands. Ruth placed the candy near her, and went back to her work. The child pulled the candy towards her, ate it, still lying on the floor, and at last fell asleep.

"Was there ever such a child?" said Ruth. "If I take her up, she'll cry and kick and scream till the walls come down. If I leave her there, she'll get cold. Well, I can but cover her up with a shawl and let her alone."

CHAPTER VII.

I SHALL skip over several years of Tangle Thread's life now, for I don't like to write about naughty children. When she was old enough to learn to read, her mother was glad, for she thought the child would be better and happier if she could amuse herself with books. She determined to give her four very short lessons every day, so as never to let her get tired. So one morning she called Tangle Thread, and taking her into her lap, she said:

"Here is a nice little book for you, and I am going to teach you to read. Don't you want to learn to read?"

"No," said Tangle Thread; "I want to play."

"Yes, you shall play very soon. But you must learn a little bit of a lesson first. And I do not like you to say 'No' when you speak to me. I wish you to be a polite little girl, and it isn't polite to speak so to your mamma."

"I don't want to be polite," said Tangle Thread.

Her mamma sighed a little, though she tried not to, and smiled as sweetly and pleasantly as ever.

"This letter is great A," said she. "See! one of his legs goes up so, and the other down, so. What did I say his name was?"

"I don't know," said Tangle Thread, in a sulky voice.

"A," said her mother. "Now say it after me —A."

"I don't want to learn to read," repeated Tangle Thread.

"But I am resolved you shall learn, my child," replied her mother. "Now say A, after me."

Tangle Thread was silent. Her mother looked at her watch. The time she had set apart for the lesson was over.

"My child," said she, "you have disobeyed me, and I must punish you. And at twelve o'clock I shall give you another lesson." Then with a heavy heart she punished the little girl, and sent her back to the nursery.

At twelve o'clock the nurse brought her home from her usual morning-walk, took off her things, brushed her hair, and led her to her mother for the second lesson, as she had been told to do.

Her mother received her with a loving word and a kiss.

"Now can you tell me the name of the letter?" she asked.

"I don't know, and I *said* I didn't know. And I don't want to learn to read."

"I think you *do* know, Tangle Thread," said her mother. "But I will tell you once more. It is A."

"I can't say A," said Tangle Thread. "And I can't say B, either. Nor C."

"Why, where did you learn your letters?" asked her mother, in great surprise. "How glad I am that you know them!"

"They're on my blocks," said Tangle Thread, in a gracious voice. "And if you'll buy me a wax doll as big as Edith May's, I'll say some more."

"I can't promise to pay you for doing what I bid you," replied her mother. "You have a dozen dolls now, and if you had one like Edith's, you would soon break it. But do not let us talk of that now. Let me hear you say D."

Half-crying, and with pouts and frowns, this second lesson was finished. Tangle Thread's mother went on faithfully to teach her naughty child, in spite of her behaviour. But when she called her to her lessons, she felt very much as people do when they go up the steps of the dentist's house

Half-crying, and with pouts and frowns, this second lesson was finished.
P. 32.

and ring his bell. Tangle Thread never came pleasantly; she almost always cried before they got through the few minutes' task; she would not half listen to what was said, and everything had to be repeated over and over again. Her book was blotted with tears, and its leaves were crumpled in her impatient hands, so that many a new one had to be bought before the end of the year. And oh! how many weary, weary hours this work she had looked forward to with pleasure cost the poor mother!

CHAPTER VIII.

When Tangle Thread could read quite well, her mamma bought for her a good many pretty little books, and a book-case in which to keep them. And one day she went out on purpose to get a silver thimble for her, that she might learn to sew. Then she fitted some work very nicely, and sat down by Tangle Thread's side, so as to show her how to hold the needle and how to take the stitches. But Tangle Thread was just as naughty about this task as she had been in learning to read. Now, if any one had said to her:

"Tangle Thread, take your needle and prick your mamma's cheeks and neck and arms all over with it," do you think the child was cruel enough to do so? No, indeed. But when she cried, and made her needle rusty with her tears; when she jerked her thread till it broke or became full of hard knots; when she pouted, and was sullen or impatient, her mother was really wounded over

and over again, and that in a tenderer spot than
cheek or arm or neck. Remember that, my child,
the next time you are tempted to behave as Tangle
Thread did, and beg God to help you to be gentle
and patient to those who take the trouble to teach
you.

Tangle Thread had also to learn to write. Then
she would not sit properly at the table, or hold
her pen as she ought; she blotted her book and
stained her fingers with ink, and kept saying:

" O dear ! I wish I didn't have to learn to
write !" or, " I wish I could hold my pen as I've
a mind."

While her mother stood over Tangle Thread
trying to teach her, she had to keep silently praying to God to give her patience with this wilful
little child. For sometimes she was tempted to
say:

" Very well; since you will not learn pleasantly,
you shall not learn at all. I will let you grow up
a dunce."

But she loved her child too well to do this, and
she loved God too well not to try to do the work
He had given her to do, in the best possible manner, leaving it to Him to make that work hard or
easy, as He thought best.

But she was so troubled with her child's con-
duct, that when she tried to read she often did not

know what book she held in her hand, and when she tried to draw or paint, her hand would tremble so that she had no pleasure in what she was doing. By degrees the piano was opened less and less frequently, the portfolio of drawings began to be neglected, and new books and magazines to lie with uncut leaves upon the table. What she studied now was the character of her child, and how best to mould and to fashion it into the likeness of Christ; and wherever she went or whatever she did, there was always a secret care gnawing at her heart. Is it so with your mother? Do you never speak that rude or impatient word to her which cuts her to the quick? When you see her sitting silent and anxious, can you say to yourself:

"Whatever it may be that is now grieving my dear mother, I *know* it is nothing *I* have said or done?"

Do not hurry over these pages without stopping to think. This book is not written merely to amuse you. It is written with the hope of touching the heart of some wilful child, of persuading it to pray day and night that God would make it docile and submissive, like Him of whom it is said:

"As a lamb before its shearers is dumb, so He opened not His mouth."

CHAPTER IX.

THERE was once a piece of coarse, black stuff, and a bright golden thread waved and rippled through it like a sunbeam.

And there was a poor, solitary woman, who had known little but trouble since the day she was born. When she was only eight years old, the parent-birds pushed her out of the nest to find home and shelter where she could. Nobody taught her to read or to write; nobody cared where she went or what she did. She wore rags for clothing, ate the coarsest food, and not enough of that; was knocked about, scolded, and abused. At last she was married. Her husband lived with her till what little money she had laid up was gone, and then ran away. After a time she heard that he was dead.

But just before he went away, God had pity on the joyless life of this poor woman, and He wove into it a golden thread. In other words, He sent a little smiling, loving child into the dark room that used to be so lonely. There wasn't much in it besides the child. While the mother lay in bed with the baby by her side, the drunken husband had broken most of the furniture to pieces with an axe. The chest of drawers that she had been so proud of, was only fit to light the fire now; and the table and the chairs were not worth much more. But what if the floor was covered with these fragments—wasn't there a live baby lying on her arm?

Little Golden Thread grew fat every minute, as good babies are apt to do. God had provided plenty of sweet milk for her, and nobody had to go out of the house to buy it when the baby was hungry. It kept coming as fast as it was wanted, just as oil kept coming into the poor woman's cruse in the Bible. But food for the mother did not come of its own accord, and it was necessary for her to do something to earn money to pay her rent with—to buy bread and potatoes and coal and clothes. She did not know, at first, how to manage it; for she must stay at home and take care of her baby, and could not go out to work as she used to do. There was a poor little seamstress who was willing to pay half-a-crown a week if she would let her come and sleep in her bed. And she came every night, when her day's labour was ended, and crept in far over toward the wall, so as to leave room for Golden Thread and her mother. Then in the morning, while the child was taking its nap, the mother would go out, with an old poker in one hand and a tin pail in the other, to rake out bits of coal from rich people's ash-barrels. Her clothes were scanty, and of all sorts of odd shapes, so that if you happened to see her from your bed-room window, half-buried in your barrel of ashes, you would hardly have been able to tell whether that queer figure was a man's or a woman's. These bits of coal helped to keep them warm, and to cook a dinner now and then.

Golden Thread had to lie on an old rug on the floor, and take care of herself most of the time. Her mother was afraid to leave her on the bed, lest she should fall off. But the child was happy on her rug, and she threw up her arms and hands and legs, and played with them, or watched her mother moving about the room, or just lay kicking and laughing and crowing and cooing. Some of her little clothes were always in the wash-tub, or else hanging on a line behind the stove, drying. This was because she had so few things, that they had to be washed every day. But she did not know or care anything about that. She went on enjoying herself just as much as if she had had a houseful of clothes; and her mother would stop now and then, look fondly down at the old rug and the little creature on it, and say half-aloud, half to herself, "Little comfort! little blessing!" and then go cheerily on with her work.

CHAPTER X.

WHEN Golden Thread had learned to creep and
to walk, it was not so safe to go out and leave her
alone as it had been.   She would get burned or
scalded, or pull the chairs over and hurt herself,
because she did not know any better than to get
into mischief.   So her mother had to wrap her up
in an old shawl, and take her with her when she
went out.   Golden Thread used to pat and kiss
her as they went along with the clothes that were
to be washed, or the coarse needlework that was
to be done.   And this made the way seem short
when it was long.   This poor woman had often to
carry a very heavy basket on one arm, with her
child on the other; and this was hard, and she
often had to stop to take breath. If Golden Thread
had fallen asleep, these sudden halts would wake
her up; then she would smile, put up her lips to
be kissed, and settle down to sleep again.   And as
soon as she was strong enough to trot along by
her mother's side, she wanted to help carry the

·basket, or the pail, or the bundle that was almost as big as herself, indeed sometimes much bigger than she was. Now, of course, she could not help at all, and yet it was very sweet to see her try, and to watch her bright face when she fancied herself of some use to her mother. Don't you remember how pleased you were when you ran to get your papa's boots for him? And how pleased *he* was, too? You see, you were like little Golden Thread when you did that.

When Golden Thread was three years old, her mother thought she must begin to leave her at home, and go out to work by the day. Ladies who wanted washing done would let her come and wash for them all day, give her plenty of good food to eat, and when she went home at night, pay her two shillings for her work. So she asked one of her neighbours to look in now and then to see how the child was getting along, made up a fire that would last till her return, put bread where Golden Thread could reach it, charged her to be a good girl, and went away. She knew that Golden Thread would stay where she was bidden, but she did not love to go and leave her all alone, and she went back twice to kiss her and to promise to' get home as early as possible. Golden Thread did not cry or fret when her mother had gone, and she heard her lock the door behind her. She ran and climbed up into a chair, to look out from the window and watch for her to come home, just as she always did when her mother went out on errands. She sat patiently and quietly a long, long time, thinking every minute she should see her mother turn the corner, and then hear her step coming up the stairs. She did not know how long a day is. By-and-by, the neighbour who had promised to look after her came up and unlocked the door, and put in her head. Golden Thread's mother had given her the key to keep while she was gone.

"O mother! is that you?" cried the lonely little child, running to the door.

"No, it's not time for your mother to be back yet. Suppose you go down and stay with me a bit?"

Golden Thread was very glad to go, and for a time she was quite happy, playing with the neighbour's children. But by-and-by they began to quarrel, and to pull each other's hair; and their mother boxed all the ears in the room, even poor Golden Thread's, without stopping to ask who was to blame, and the poor little thing was very glad to be taken home again to her own room. The fire had begun to get low, and the neighbour put on more coal before she went away. Golden Thread made believe iron when she was left alone, but this made her arms ache, and then she made houses with the clothes-pins. Then dinner-time came, and she ate her bread and drank some water, and climbed up to watch once more for her mother. Dear me! what a joyful sound it was, to hear her come toiling up the stairs! They hugged and kissed each other so many times, and it was so nice!

"Poor little soul!" said her mother; "it was lonesome while its mother was gone!"

"But you've come now!" cried Golden Thread; and she forgot all the long hours, and was just as happy as a little bird.

And the tired mother forgot how tired she was, and she put on the tea-kettle and a saucepan, and began to get the little one's supper. She had had hers, and now all she thought of was giving something warm to her child, who had been so sweet and contented with her bread and water all day.

"See," said she, "this pretty white egg. I am going to boil it for you. And you shall have a drop of milk and a bit of sugar and a cup of tea to-night. And mother'll make you a slice of toast." What a feast after a long, lonely day!

"Mother, do rich people have such nice suppers?" asked Golden Thread, hopping round her and looking gaily on.

"Dear me! bless the child!" said her mother;

and she laughed all to herself, and felt a good deal happier than many rich folks put together.

So Golden Thread sat up to the table and had her warm supper. Her tea was make-believe tea, made of water with a little milk in it; but she had it in a real tea-cup, and the egg wasn't a make-believe egg by any means.

"I'm going again to-morrow to the same place," said her mother; "and you must be a good child, and not fret for mother."

"No, I won't fret one bit," said Golden Thread. "And when you're a big girl, I'll buy you a great big egg and cook it for your supper."

"Why, I'm a big girl now," said her mother. Then they both laughed a good deal, and by-and-by it was time to go to bed. When Golden Thread had fallen asleep, her mother put on her hood and shawl, and went out to spend the money she had earned that day. She bought a little coal and a loaf of bread, and three pennyworth of tea, and some meal. Some of the meal was to be boiled next morning for the child's breakfast; and the coal was to keep her from freezing through the wintry day.

"Wait upon me as soon as you can," she said to the grocer of whom she bought her tea; "for I've locked my little girl up alone in the room, and I'm so afraid of fires when it comes night."

"It's a pretty risky thing to lock a child up, day or night," replied the grocer. "There's no telling how many come to their death that way every year. You see, they get lonesome, and they fall to playing with the fire, or with matches."

"My little girl never does such things," said the woman.

"That doesn't prove she never will do them, some time," persisted the grocer. "Children's all just alike. And it's my opinion they all make a point of getting into all the mischief they can. Don't lock 'em up in rooms by themselves, *I* say."

"That's my doctrine too," said another man who stood by. "Besides, it's a piece of cruelty. Children wasn't made to live alone by the day."

"I don't know what else we poor folks are to do," said Golden Thread's mother. She caught up her basket, and hastened away to see that the child was safe.

CHAPTER XI.

GOLDEN THREAD spent a great many such days as the one I have told you about. How would you like to be locked into the room and left alone all day? Do you think you should cry?

At last Golden Thread was old enough to go to school, and then her long, lonely days were over. It is hard work to learn to read, but it isn't half so hard as to stay by yourself all day. So Golden Thread was very happy to stand by her teacher's side and be taught her letters. There were a great many children in the school, and many of them were naughty, tiresome children. They teased their teacher, and gave her a great deal of trouble, so that she often got quite out of patience, and would speak sharply to them, or even shake them. She even got out of patience with our good little Golden Thread, because she did not learn faster; and one day she spoke quite roughly to her, and said:

"You are as stupid as an owl!"

The tears came into Golden Thread's eyes, but

she looked up sweetly into her teacher's face, and said: "Why, Miss Bacon! you called me an owl!"

"I did not mean to call you so," replied the teacher. "You must forgive me for speaking so rudely. You are my best child, and if all the rest were like you, I should not lose my temper so."

When Golden Thread's mother came home that night, with her limbs aching, and her hands all wrinkled and puckered with hot water, how pleased she was to hear her dear child say:

"My teacher says I am her best child!"

Indeed, the poor woman did not creep home to a dark and gloomy room in these days, as she used to do before she had any child. As she passed swiftly through the streets, she knew that Golden Thread would have the fire burning cheerfully, the room nicely swept, the candle lighted, and the little low chair waiting for her. And what was more, she knew that the moment she opened the door, she should hear the joyful cry, "Oh! here you come, mother!" and that two arms would be round her neck and twenty kisses on her cheek before she had time to take off her things. Oh! it is so pleasant to have somebody glad to see you when you get home! Sailors on the sea think so, and soldiers in their tents think so, and so all mothers think who have little Golden Threads watching and waiting for them.

"I wish I might bring home to you some of the good things I see wasted every day," said the mother. "Or, that I could go without half my dinner, so that you could have it."

Golden Thread looked quite surprised.

"Why, mother, I have plenty to eat!" said she. "Some children have to go a-begging. They are worse off than I am."

"Well, you haven't plenty of clothes, at any rate. I wish you had. Then you wouldn't have to lie in bed while I wash and dry what few old things you have."

Then Golden Thread laughed, and said: "But it is so nice that I've got some clothes, and don't have to lie in bed all the time. And pretty soon I shall be a big girl, and can help you work, and we shall have lots of clothes."

Yet down in the depths of little Golden Thread's heart there lay a good many wants and wishes that she never told of. There are always such wishes in the hearts of those who are poor, or only pretty well off. Some great agitation throws them to the surface, and friends see them with astonishment, not dreaming of their existence until now. Just so, all sorts of plants are growing down in the depths of the sea. But it needs a great wind or storm to tear them loose from the rocks, and toss them to the surface.

CHAPTER XII.

GOLDEN THREAD'S mother kept on working very hard, and by degrees she was able to get good warm clothing for herself and her child. She bought a new chest of drawers and some chairs and a table, and their room looked more like a nice pleasant home than ever. But hard work in all sorts of weather, now in freezing cold, now in long summer days, requires a good deal of health and strength, and this poor woman began to lose hers. Now and then, instead of going out to earn money, she had to stay at home to rest, and then what she had been saving had to be used up. At last, one day, she fell from a ladder on which she was standing, and the pail of whitewash she had been using overturned, and poured its contents all over her. Her eyes were filled, and so was her mouth, and she could hardly breathe or see. Some of the servants in the house where she was at work helped her to get up and wipe the white-wash from her face, but they could not cure her

E

eyes, which burned like fire. One of them led her home, where she spent the night in great pain and anxiety. In the morning, Golden Thread could not run gaily to school, as usual. She must lead her half-blind mother to a dispensary. Do you know what a dispensary is? If not, ask your mother, and she will tell you. The poor woman was given something with which to cool her eyes, but it did little good; and she sat with folded hands, she who had always been so busy! Golden Thread made the fire and got the breakfast, and swept the room, and she said everything she could think of to comfort her mother.

But the poor woman needed a great deal of comfort. She knew that if she lost her eyes, she could not work any more to earn money for herself and her child. They would be turned out of their pleasant little home, and have to go to the Alms-house. When she said so, Golden Thread answered:

"But won't they be good to us in the Alms-house?"

"You don't know what you are talking about, poor thing," said her mother. "And I'm glad you don't. And to think of my being blind, and not able to walk another step!"

"But you've got me to lead you, mother," said Golden Thread. "It isn't so bad as if you hadn't any little girl like me."

" No, I know it isn't. But if I am blind, I never shall see your face again."

" But you can feel it with your hands, and that's most as good," said Golden Thread. " And I shall never leave you; no, not one minute. And pretty soon I shall be able to read to you. I'll read such beautiful stories. All about kings and soldiers and battles and giants. There's lots of stories in the Bible."

" Dear me! the child would bring a dead man to life!" said the mother. " And I am an ungrateful creature not to be thinking of my mercies instead of sitting here groaning. Why, if I had to choose which I'd lose, this child or my two eyes, it would come dreadful hard, but I'd choose to keep the child."

So many days passed, but the injured eyes were no better, and all the neighbours came in to see the poor woman and to give their advice. One wanted her to try this thing and another that, and at last they told of a woman who knew a great deal about the eye, and would be sure to cure the worst case. Golden Thread danced for joy when she heard this; for she believed all she heard, like other little children. She could hardly wait till her mother was got ready to set off to visit this wonderful person who was to cure her eyes. She led her carefully and tenderly along the street, just as you would lead your little baby-sister if you were allowed to take her out. The woman-doctor looked at the eyes and made great promises, and in return for her advice she took fourteen shillings from the widow's hard-working hands. And she took fourteen shillings a good many times after this, till all the money the poor woman had was gone. And at the end of the visits her eyes were almost gone, too.

CHAPTER XIII.

THESE were hard times. The cupboard that held all their treasures was sold; by-and-by the little clock, that used to tick so cheerfully, went where the cupboard did; then the mother's warm shawl was pawned; then Golden Thread's best frock, that she wore at Sunday-school; then other things, one after another, till they and their room looked as forlorn as a room could that had Golden Thread in it, and as Golden Thread could, while always wearing her sweet, cheery smiles.

But winter was coming on; and winter wants many things that summer can do without. It wants those blankets that are at the pawnbroker's; those thick shawls and petticoats, plenty of coal, plenty of warm food.

"Mother," said Golden Thread, "if rich people knew how poor we are, wouldn't they give us something?"

"Yes, I dare say; but I never begged."

"But there was a lady said she would give us

cold pieces if we would come for them. Is it begging to go?"

"Why, if I ever get well, I could do something to pay for them," replied her mother. "You're hungry, poor thing, I know you are. Come, I'll go with you. But it comes hard," she added, for her courage failed her, and she sat down again, and pressed both hands on her eyes, to keep back the tears that would have scalded them.

"Never mind, mother," said Golden Thread, "I am not *very* hungry. And there's my best shoes left; maybe we could get something for them."

"Well, we'll try," said her mother. They put on their scanty shawls and went out.

Golden Thread held her mother's hand fast in hers, and led her carefully along, looking on all sides to see that she was not run over—picking out the dry places, and every now and then speaking a word of love and good cheer.

Walking slowly along in this way, Golden Thread observed a lady very richly dressed, leading by the hand a little girl younger than herself. The child was made on a very tiny scale. Her hands and feet were so small, that you could not help wondering at them; and her very red cheeks were on such a cunning little face, that you would have said they were doll's cheeks, if the eyes and the mouth hadn't such a wise and knowing way with them. She was pulling very hard on the hand that held hers, trying to get away. Hear what she says, and perhaps you will know who she is:

"If I can't have plum-cake and coffee, I don't want any party. Edith has plum-cake, and she drinks two cups of coffee. When I am a big woman, I mean to have just what I've a mind."

"Do you see that little girl across the street?" asked her mother. "See how miserably she is dressed. Look at her poor feet. Her shoes are so old, that she can hardly keep them on. And the poor woman she is leading has a bandage over her eyes. Do you think that little girl teazes for rich cake and coffee? Do you think, if I should invite her to come to our house to lunch, she would cry for things I did not give her?"

"She would be afraid to cry," replied Tangle Thread; "and I dare say she is a bad girl, and her mother is only making believe blind. Gertrude says the streets are full of impostors."

Tangle Thread was so pleased that she had said a big word, that her ill-humour began to give way.

"I'll run and ask them if they're impostors," said she; "and if they say they're not, I'll give them a shilling," she added, tossing up her little bit of a head.

And before her mother had time to answer, she ran towards Golden Thread. who had stopped to pull up her shoes that kept slipping from her feet. Many carriages and heavy carts and stages were passing, and the child was in the midst of them before her mother had recovered from her surprise at her flight. A moment more, and she would have been thrown down, and perhaps killed. But Golden Thread pulled off her old shoes, ran quickly to the middle of the crossing, and snatched up the little figure in her own big arms.

"Put me down, you old girl, you!" cried Tangle Thread, frightened and angry. "Put me down, I say! I've got as many feet as you have!"

By this time her mother had reached them.

"Thank you, little girl," said she, looking at Golden Thread—"thank you with all my heart. You are a brave child, to run in among the horses and carriages to save this foolish little thing. But is that thin shawl warm enough, this cold day? And are not your feet half-frozen?"

"Oh! I don't mind it," said Golden Thread, smiling, and slipping her feet into her old shoes.

"And is this your mother?" asked the lady, looking with pity at the bandaged eyes.

"Yes, ma'am; but I lead her," replied Golden Thread. "She's hurt her eyes, and can't see so well as she used."

"Do you see that house at the corner?" asked the lady. "Well, I live there, and I wish you

"Do you see that house at the corner?"—P. 56.

would come and see me to-morrow morning. Will you let her come?" she asked in a gentle voice, turning to Golden Thread's mother.

"The child's hardly decent, ma'am," said the poor woman.

"She looks very clean, I'm sure," said the lady.

"Very well, if you're kind enough to think so, ma'am," replied the woman.

So they bid each other good-by, and each passed on their way; only Golden Thread and Tangle Thread looked back at each other several times.

"What a nice, pleasant-looking little girl!" said Tangle Thread's mother. "And O, my child! how thankful we ought to be to God for saving you when you were in such danger! How could you run across the street in that reckless way? You know how often I have told you never to do it. But I won't say any more about it. I am too thankful that no harm has come to you."

"Should you cry if I should be killed?" asked Tangle Thread. "If I had been killed, you wouldn't have had any little girl to tease you."

"O my darling child! how little you know how your mother loves you! If you only could *begin* to know, what a different child you would be!"

Tangle Thread's proud little heart melted a little, and she said in a low voice:

"I won't tease for plum-cake and coffee again.

I'll have just what you want me to have. And I am going to invite that little girl to my party. I don't think she's an impostor."

Her mother smiled, and would gladly have caught her child in her arms and covered her with kisses, as they entered the house together. But Tangle Thread would not have allowed herself to be caressed for making one civil speech. She was too proud for that. So they went in together, and were both full of business all day.

Golden Thread and her mother went on, meanwhile, to the pawnbroker's, where they pawned the shoes. With the money thus gained they bought a bit of bread, and hungry as they were, ate it on the way home.

"What do you suppose that rich lady wants me to come there for, mother?" asked Golden Thread.

"I suppose she wants to give you something, because you picked up her little girl for her."

"She must be a very nice lady, then. It only took me a minute to snatch up the little girl."

"Yes, but you might have got run over and killed in that one minute. And then what would have become of your poor old mother?"

Golden Thread was silent. But after a while she said: "I don't believe God would take away your eyes and your little girl both at once. And if that kind lady gives me as much as a shilling,

I'll buy a little piece of beef with it. The doctor you went to first said you wasn't at all strong, and ought to eat beef."

"Much he knows where it's to come from!" said the mother. "But that lady won't give you money, child. How should she, not knowing but that I would take it from you and spend it in drink?"

CHAPTER XIV.

THE next morning, very early, Golden Thread washed her face and hands, and combed her hair, and was going to set off at once to make the promised visit. But her mother said:

"You must not go these three hours. The lady won't be up this long while, and then there's her breakfast. It will take a good deal longer to eat it than it takes us to eat our bit of dry bread."

Golden Thread tried to wait in patience, but it was ten o'clock when her mother at last let her set off. She was taken up stairs, where her new friend sat by a cheerful fire, with Tangle Thread by her side.

"Come in," said the lady; "come to the fire and warm yourself. Have you had your breakfast?"

"O yes, ma'am! a good while ago," said Golden Thread, trying not to look round her at the beautiful things in the room, but looking in spite of herself.

"If you had your breakfast long ago, I dare say you could eat some more by this time. Or would you rather have something to take home, so as to share it with the rest?"

"There isn't anybody but mother," said Golden Thread.

"And she is almost blind, isn't she?"

"Her eyes were almost burnt up with white-wash," replied Golden Thread; "and since then she can't work as she used. If she could, she wouldn't let me go into a lady's house with such shoes on," she added, looking down at her miserable feet: "she says she hopes you will excuse it."

"To be sure, to be sure," said the lady, drawing a little chair to the fire. "Sit down, my child, and tell me what is your name?"

"Mother calls me her little Golden Thread. But that isn't my real name. My real name is ———"

"Never mind; I am sure it isn't so pretty as the one by which your mother calls you. And now, Golden Thread, do you know why I asked you to come here to-day?"

"No, ma'am."

"Well, I wanted to ask you, for one thing, if you were going to have a good many little girls come to see you, what would you give them to eat?"

Golden Thread smiled and looked down. At last she said:

"Why, if I had plenty of roasted potatoes, with butter on them, I'd give them as many as they liked. Roasted potatoes are very nice, if you have butter with them."

"And nothing else?"

"And maybe I'd give every one a piece of cake. I mean, if I had any cake. But I shouldn't, you know, ma'am."

The lady looked at Tangle Thread and smiled, and Tangle Thread smiled too, for she was thinking, as her mother was, of the sponge-cake, and maccaroons, and kisses, and candies, and ice-cream that had been ordered for her party. And which she had pouted about, and said she wouldn't have, unless there was wedding-cake and coffee!

"And now, Golden Thread," said the lady, "I should like you to tell me what of all things you want most. For I feel very grateful to you, and it will be a great pleasure to me to give you something."

Golden Thread smiled, and looked thoughtfully into the fire. Dear me! she wanted so many things most!

Then the lady said:

"In this deep bureau-drawer, I keep things to give away. You would laugh if you could see

what queer things I keep in it. T...
and clothing, and shoes and stocking...

"Oh! is there a pair of shoes the...
Golden Thread, jumping up.

"Why didn't you say a big wax doll?"
Tangle Thread. "Mamma would just as lief g...
you a doll as not."

"There are no shoes large enough for you in
the drawer," said the lady. "Come, what would
you like next best to shoes?"

"Perhaps there's stockings," suggested the
child. "Mother says warm stockings are good
for chilblains."

"Oh! there are larger things in the drawer
than stockings. Choose once more."

"There never could be a shawl big enough for
mother?"

The lady rose, opened the drawer, and took
thence a thick woollen shawl.

"Like this?" she asked.

"Oh, how nice!" cried Golden Thread. "Mother
is so cold since she got sick. But have I been
begging? oh! have I been begging?" she cried,
looking alarmed. "Did I ask for a shawl for
mother? And I was never thinking of a big warm
shawl like that."

"Perhaps you were thinking of a little warm
one, like this," said the lady, almost crying with

out so many of the
t this is just large
ı give the other to

thank you !'' cried

; in the drawer,''
into a chair and
-books, dolls, reti-

____ tnings here ?'' asked
__ mother, surprised.

"I put them there my own self," replied Tangle Thread. "They are for the little girl. And I should like to have her take off her things and stay here and play with me."

"I left mother all alone, and I must go now," said Golden Thread.

"Stop a minute," said the lady. "These thick night-gowns are for you."

"Why, I never had any night-gowns," said Golden Thread, with great surprise and pleasure. "What *will* mother say ?"

"And in this bundle you will find a good many other such things."

"Why, I had to lie in bed while my things were washed! I'll go straight home and show all these to mother. What *will* she say ?"

The lady smiled, and Tangle Thread looked almost as much astonished as Golden Thread. She drew near, and whispered:

"But why don't you ask my mamma for a big doll? And some cake and candy, and nuts and raisins?"

Golden Thread was speechless. Was she the sort of child to ask for dolls and cake and candy, while her mother sat half-blind, half-frozen, half-starved at home?

"Oh!" she cried, bursting into tears, "it isn't nice things we want. It's bread and meat and fire!"

Tangle Thread rushed out of the room and up stairs to Ruth.

"Give me all my money, quick!" said she; "there's a little girl down stairs that wants some bread and meat and fire."

"Oh! your mamma won't let you give to beggars," said Ruth.

"She isn't a beggar any more than you are!" cried Tangle Thread, angrily. "And I will have my money. Get it, this instant!"

"I'm not to give you things unless you ask me in a proper way."

"I will have my money!" said Tangle Thread; and she climbed up and opened the upper bureau-drawer, and began to turn over the things there in search of her purse.

F

"Don't toss over your nice clean collars in that way," said Ruth. "Your purse is not in that drawer, and you'll not find it if you look all day."

Tangle Thread burst into loud and angry cries. She took out her nice collars and aprons, and threw them one by one to the floor, and was trampling them under her feet when her mamma suddenly entered the room.

The happy moments she had spent with Golden Thread were over, and she stood in the door with that sorrowful, grieved look that was now almost always on her face. She did not say a word, but taking the angry child by the hand, she led her down stairs to her own room, and seated herself opposite to her in silence.

CHAPTER XV

WERE you ever disappointed in your life? When you were going into the country to spend the day, and it began to rain just as you were all ready to set off, how did you feel? And when you were invited to a Christmas-tree, and had talked about nothing else for a week, how did you behave when your mamma said you had too severe a cold to go, and all the other children went without you? You were disappointed, and very likely cried more or less about it. Well, Tangle Thread's mother was disappointed that just as her child seemed gentler and sweeter than usual, her goodness lasted so little while. You know just how she felt as she sat there looking at Tangle Thread sobbing with anger. But no, you do not know, and you never will, till you grow up and have some little children of your own.

Meanwhile Golden Thread had gone home, and one of the maids went with her, as she was directed to do, with a basket on her arm and some money in her pocket. With the money she was to buy shoes and stockings, that Golden Thread was to put on and wear home.

"But I've a pair of shoes at the pawnbroker's," said Golden Thread.

"Never mind, I'm to do as I'm told," said the maid. "If you ever get your other shoes back, they'll maybe do for Sundays."

"Look at me, mother!" cried Golden Thread, running in with her stout shoes on, and making all the noise she could. "Lift up your bandage just a minute, and see what I've got. Shoes and stockings and shawls and nightgowns and petticoats; and the lady says she's coming to see you. And here are roasted potatoes right out of the oven, and butter to eat with them! O mother! I didn't mean to beg for them."

The poor mother looked so bewildered and so ready to cry, that the maid thought it best to set the basket on the table, and to slip out as quietly as she could. As soon as she had gone, Golden Thread flew into her mother's arms.

"Oh! it was such a nice lady!" said she. "She is coming to see you, and says you must go to her doctor, and let him see your eyes. And she told me to tell you not to be troubled, for you would not be left to suffer when you were not fit to work."

The poor woman shook her head. " I cannot take all these things," said she. " I never can pay for them, and I haven't been used to having things I didn't work for."

Golden Thread stood silent, for she did not know what to say.

" At any rate, you'll eat some of the potatoes, won't you, mother?" she asked. And she began taking them from the basket. " Why, there's a piece of roast meat here!" she cried. " O mother! it will do you so much good! And there's enough to last a week!"

They sat down, hungry and thankful, to this little dinner, and then they looked at the shawls, the shoes, and all the other treasures.

" I can't think of keeping them," said the poor woman again. " Unless, indeed, the lady will let me come and work for her whenever I get well."

" The lady is very rich," said Golden Thread, looking down at her shoes. " And she said herself that my old shoes were not fit to wear."

Her mother made no answer, but looked again and again at the thick shawls, and at last laid everything carefully away on the bed.

" I haven't got down quite so low as all this comes to," said she. " Begging is a trade I wasn't brought up to. We must not keep these things.

Just as soon as my eyes get well, I shall be able to earn what we need."

" Maybe if you'd seen the lady as long as I did, mother, you wouldn't mind taking presents from her. But I'll do just as you say. You are not angry with me, are you?"

" Angry with you? Bless your heart! No, indeed. If I'm angry with anybody, it's with myself, for getting that fall and spoiling my eyes."

CHAPTER XVI.

WHILE this was going on in the one small room in which Golden Thread lived, poor little Tangle Thread sat crying before her mamma. She was crying with anger, and when spoken to, she made no answer, unless it was by crying more loudly, and by kicking against the chair on which she sat. So at last her mamma rose quietly and went away into another room. There she threw herself down upon her knees, hid her face in her hands, and burst into tears. Then she prayed long and earnestly to God to touch the heart of her child. When she returned to her room, Tangle Thread had stopped crying, and looked tired. Indeed, she was both tired and ashamed. She wished she hadn't been so angry, and that she could tell her mamma so. But it would have been easier to have a tooth out than to tell her secret thoughts to anybody.

"Come here, my child," said her mother tenderly, and holding out her hand.

Tangle Thread rose slowly, and walked to her mother's side.

"I am not going to say anything to you about your behaviour," said her mother. "I have said everything I had to say a great many times already And I am not going to punish you, either. I am quite tired of that. I can hardly remember a day in your life that I have not had to punish you in some way. But I will tell you to-morrow what I intend to do."

She spoke in a gentle, loving, but very sad tone, and Tangle Thread saw that her eyes were red with crying. She never had felt so miserable in her life. What a pity that she did not throw herself into her mamma's arms, tell her how sorry she felt, and promise to try, with God's help, to be a better child! But she did not say a word, and very soon the carriage was ordered, and she saw her mamma drive off. She went back to the nursery and tried to play with her dolls, but they did not comfort her. Then she took down *The Fairchild Family*, and read a little here and there in that favourite book.

Meanwhile her mother drove from place to place, making inquiries about Golden Thread's mother. She heard nothing ill of her anywhere. Everybody said she was a hard-working, industrious woman. So then she drove to the house where the poor woman lived. All the neighbours ran to the windows to look at the carriage, and some of them directed her to the room she was seeking.

"O mother! it's the nice lady!" cried Golden Thread, as she opened the door, on hearing her gentle knock.

"I have come to see you on account of your eyes," said the lady, kindly. "I want you to tell me all about your accident, and what has been done for your eyes since they were injured."

Golden Thread's mother was glad to tell her story to so kind a listener, and by degrees a good many things came out that she did not mean to tell.

"I will take you to see an oculist, if you are willing to go," said the lady. "I have the carriage at the door, on purpose, and there is plenty of time before dark."

The poor woman coloured, and was silent. At last she said:

"I thank you, ma'am, with all my heart. But I am not decent to go with a lady like you. If you would please to give me a bit of a note to the doctor, my little girl could lead me to his house."

"It is too far. Besides, I want to see him myself. Your shawl will nearly cover you, and I'm sure your dress is clean and tidy."

"Do go," whispered Golden Thread. "Do go, mother."

"I was going to say, ma'am, speaking of the shawl and things, that I am grateful for them; but I can't think of taking them unless you will let me do something for you. I can wash and iron, and scrub and scour, and I understand whitewashing; and I can get in coal and sweep off the walks."

"Not now that you are nearly blind!" said the lady.

"Why, no, ma'am, I can't say that I can see to do much of anything now; but I hope to get well."

"The first thing, then, is to see what the doctor says," replied the lady; "and I promise to give you work as soon as you are able to do it. So get ready, and we'll go at once. Put on your shawl, too, Golden Thread," she added, "for of course you are to go with us."

You should have seen Golden Thread's face as she led her mother down the stairs and helped her into the carriage. Driving off in a carriage as if they were queens! Well, if it was a dream, what a delightful dream it was!

The doctor said the poor eyes were in a sad state, what with the whitewash and the quack medicine. But he thought they would be well in time. He spoke kindly and cheerfully to the poor woman, who felt as if a great, heavy stone had been lifted off her heart.

"And now," said the lady, as she set her down

at her own door, "I have one thing more to say to you. Suppose I should be very ill several months, not able to turn myself in bed, and needing constant care day and night. I should have to have a nurse, and I should take all her time and strength and patience. Now, I should pay her all she asked, and perhaps more. But could I really pay her with money, so as not to have any reason to feel grateful to her for all she had done and all she had suffered for me?"

"Why, no, ma'am, maybe not," said the poor woman, wondering what was coming next.

"Well, if I could never repay her, then I must always feel under obligation to her. I could, in fact, only repay her by nursing *her* through just such illness. But I should not be unhappy on that account. I love to feel obliged to people. I love to feel grateful to God for His goodness to me, and I love to feel grateful to kind friends for their goodness. And I want you to love to have me do all I can for you in this time of your trouble. Anybody can refuse a favour, but it isn't everybody who knows how to accept one nobly and freely. But you must try, for my sake, and for His sake who bids His children to minister to each other as they would to Him."

So saying, the lady allowed Golden Thread and her mother to alight from the carriage, and the

coachman handed them from under his seat such
a big bundle, that they could hardly get it up
stairs. And when they got there, they did not
know their own room. There was such a fire
burning; and the bureau had come back, and so
had the table and the chairs and the clock. And
when they opened the big bundle, there were blankets and a warm quilt, and shoes and stockings
for the mother, and flannel petticoats, and a woollen dress. And when she tried to put on a pair
of the stockings, there was something hard in
each toe, and the hard thing proved to be a gold
sovereign, with which to buy coal and food and
medicine all through this strait!

"Are you going to send all these things back,
mother?" asked Golden Thread, anxiously, for she
had not understood the lady's talk with her mother.

"Send them back! No, indeed! I am going
to keep them, and be grateful for them!" was the
answer.

Then Golden Thread was so glad she did not
know what to do, and she threw herself down on
the floor and rolled, like a ball, across the room.
And they put away their treasures nicely in the
drawers, and Golden Thread went out and bought
a candle to eat their supper by.

CHAPTER XVII.

THE next morning Tangle Thread's mother said to her: "I had a plan in my mind yesterday, which I do not approve of, now that I have had more time to think it over. Do you want to know what it was?"

"If it was about me, I do," said Tangle Thread.

"Well, I had half a mind to send you to spend a week with that little girl who was here yesterday."

"What, that little golden girl?"

"Little Golden Thread—yes. I thought it might do you good to see how poor people live, and to watch that nice, pleasant child at her work. But on the whole, I cannot get courage to let you go."

"Why not, mamma? I want to go. I am tired of always being in this house."

"No, I dare not trust you. You might take cold, or get into trouble of some sort."

It was just like Tangle Thread to begin to cry, and to want to go because her mamma did not wish it. So she fancied herself much injured because she could not have her own way.

"I have to play all alone," said she. "I never have any one to play with."

"Not little Gertrude?" asked her mother.

"Gertrude gets all my toys, and she won't play anything I like. She just sits and sings to my wax doll as if it was alive. Do let me go, mamma."

Her mother could hardly help smiling.

At this moment her father entered the room. He looked at Tangle Thread with displeasure, and said :

"I shall really have to send you away if you behave in this manner. You weary your mamma's life out with such constant teasing."

"I was just telling her that I had been thinking of sending her to spend a week with a poor woman I know of. But instead of being alarmed at the prospect, she is quite vexed because I will not let her go."

"Is the woman trustworthy? Does she live in a decent place?" asked the father; "for I am not sure it would not be a good thing for Tangle Thread to be sent away among strangers."

"I really begin to think so," said her mamma.

Then Tangle Thread suddenly changed her mind, and began to think she did not want to go.

"They are not nice people," said she, "and they have no meat or bread or fire. I would rather stay at home."

"I was quite in earnest in what I said," urged her father. "·A little girl who will not try to be gentle and good, and who, after so many years, continues so wilful, ought not to be treated like other little girls. If she makes her home unhappy, she ought not to stay there."

So saying, he took his hat and went out.

"I never saw your father so displeased," said Tangle Thread's mother. "I am afraid that he will really send you away. We know of a lady in the country who takes little girls, and she would be quite willing to take you."

"I wasn't any naughtier than usual," said Tangle Thread. "I don't see why I should be sent away just for fretting a little bit."

."Your father was thinking of all your naughty ways ever since you were born; and perhaps he thinks that some one else will manage you better than your mother can. But, O my poor child! nobody will love you as I do, and you will miss the love. Your heart will ache for it day and night."

Tangle Thread sighed. It is easy to be naughty, but it's hard, too.

" I won't tease you any more," said she. " It isn't very nice to tease people. I can do anything I've a mind. I can be good, and I can be naughty."

" Don't say so, my dear. Say you can be good if Jesus will help you ; for there's no use in trying unless He helps you."

" If I can't be good all by myself, I don't want to be good at all," said Tangle Thread. " You destroy all my ambition."

She was so pleased with herself for having made this great speech, that her little tightly-packed body almost seemed to swell with the pride it was hardly big enough to hold. She went to the nursery lost in thought.

" I can be good, if I've a mind," she said to herself. " I've a great mind to begin. Then everybody will be so astonished. They'll say they never saw such a sweet little girl. That's what people say about good children—they say they're sweet. And I can be sweet, if I've a mind."

These thoughts were so pleasing, that she laughed aloud.

" What are you laughing at ?" asked Ruth.

Tangle Thread blushed and started. " I wasn't laughing," said she.

" Indeed you were," said the nurse.

" I was not. Or if I was, you needn't be asking about it ! I can laugh if I choose."

"She's out of humour, and I won't say anything to vex her," thought Ruth. "I did provoke her yesterday, and I wish I hadn't."

"I've been looking everywhere for your purse," said she. "I was sorry that I did not help you look for it. But I had such a toothache, I could not bear to move. And you'll never guess where I found it. Why, in one of your boots, under the bed."

"Oh! I remember now. I played that my boot was a ship, and I put my purse on board for cargo. I am so glad I've found it. Let's go out now and give some money to that little girl."

"We must see what your mamma says, first. And I doubt if she lets you give so much money to one person."

"Yes, she will. She likes generous people."

"But what will you do when all your money is gone?"

"Oh! papa will give me plenty more."

"Then I don't call it generous to give it away. You wouldn't do it if you were not sure he would give you more."

Tangle Thread was silent. But after a minute she ran down to her mamma. She found her writing.

"Mamma!" said she, "mamma!"

"Do not interrupt me now; I am busy," said her mother.

"But, mamma, I want——"

Her mother put her gently away.

"I should think you might listen," said Tangle Thread, reproachfully.

Her mother looked up. "I was making up the week's accounts," said she, "and you have disturbed me so, that I shall have to go all over them again. Go away now, and come again in half an hour."

"But you've stopped now, and——"

"Go, my child," said her mother. "You must learn to obey."

Tangle Thread went. But it was not a "sweet little girl" who ran from the room with a flushed face.

"I'll go up into the attic, and stay there till I freeze to death," she said to herself. "Then mamma will wish she hadn't teased me so. Oh! she'll be sorry enough when she sees me lying there cold and dead!"

The attic was not a very agreeable place on this wintry day. Tangle Thread soon became tired of pouting there alone. So she determined not to freeze, but to starve to death; a resolution that she kept till supper-time, when she put it off till next day.

CHAPTER XVIII.

In half an hour her mother sent for her.

"I am at leisure now," said she; "what were you going to say?"

"I want to know if I can go to see that little girl, and give her all my money?"

"I have given her all she needs for the present," replied her mother. "But I am going to see them now, and if you wish to go with me, you can run and get ready."

Tangle Thread hesitated. At last she went up to be dressed, and she slipped the purse into her pocket.

They found Golden Thread and her mother quite cheerful and happy. Their room looked clean and pleasant; and the two children sat apart while their mothers conversed together, and had a little chat of their own.

"Where are your toys?" asked Tangle Thread.

"I have none," said Golden Thread.

"What have you done with them, then?"

"Oh! I never had any to speak of. When I was a little girl, mother made me a rag-baby; but I gave it away, long ago."

"But what do you do all day, if you have no toys?"

"I help mother. I wash the dishes, and I sweep the floor; and I can knit. I knit almost a whole stocking once."

"Can you read? Have you any books?"

"I can't read very well. I have to stay at home from school to take care of mother now."

"Why doesn't she teach you, then?"

"Oh! she's almost blind. Besides, she doesn't know how to read herself."

Tangle Thread was speechless with surprise. A grown-up woman not know how to read!

"Mamma knows everything," said she, "and she teaches me. And one of these days I shall know as much as she does. But I am afraid she won't go to heaven unless she gives you more money. She ought to give you money to buy ever so many toys with. But I've got some money of my own, and you shall have it all. You must buy a large doll and a cradle."

"But does your mamma know about it?" asked Golden Thread, half pleased and half frightened.

"No, she doesn't. It says in the Bible, that

you should not let your left hand know what your right hand does. So of course I don't want her to know about it." And Tangle Thread felt very virtuous indeed, as she put the purse into Golden Thread's hand.

By this time her mamma was ready to go; and when they were in the carriage again, she said:

"How do you feel about spending a week with that poor blind woman and her child? You know you could help them pare potatoes and wash dishes, and make their bed, and sweep."

"You are laughing at me, mamma," said Tangle Thread.

"And you may laugh at me, too, if you like," answered her mamma; "but I have another plan, now. Golden Thread cannot go to school while her mother is so helpless, and I have been thinking how it would answer to let her come every day to our house to be taught."

"Who would teach her?"

"I thought you would."

Tangle Thread could not conceal her smile of pride and pleasure. She sat up as straight as possible, and said:

"I should like that dearly."

"But you must make up your mind to find it quite a task. At first it will be pleasant, but after the novelty wears off, you will often find it irksome. But I want you to feel that you were not placed in this world just to amuse yourself and have a good time. I want you to do some things that are tiresome, and that require labour and patience."

" When may I begin ?"

" To - morrow or next day. I have already spoken to the child's mother about it."

CHAPTER XIX.

TANGLE THREAD went to bed full of ambitious schemes. She forgot that it was not Golden Thread's fault that, though two years older than herself, she could not read well. She forgot who had given her her own great readiness to learn, and yet what impatience she had always shown at her tasks.

Next morning at the appointed hour Golden Thread made her appearance.

" My mother says I ought not to have taken this money," said she, placing the purse in Tangle Thread's hand. " She says I am to say I am very sorry I was such a foolish child."

Tangle Thread's mother looked at her little daughter with surprise.

" Did you give her your purse, after all?" she asked.

" Yes, mamma," replied Tangle Thread, in a firm voice. " The Bible says : ' Blessed is he that considereth the poor.' "

" But what does it say about obedience to parents? O, Tangle Thread! what shall I do with you?"

She sank back into a chair, almost ill. Golden Thread stood looking on, surprised and troubled, and was very glad to be told that she might run home, as there would be no lessons that day.

On hearing her story, her mother was greatly shocked.

" No wonder that lady looks so sorrowful," said she. " I thought she had some trouble on her mind."

" Oh! but her little girl will never do so again," said Golden Thread. " She wouldn't like to make her mother turn so pale again."

" Ah!" thought the poor woman, " I've had a sorrowful, hard life; and if I get well, I've got to go on working just so as long as I live. But what of it? I've got the best child that ever was. A child that never crossed me in anything, nor ever spoke a rough word to me. There isn't anything God could have given a poor, lonely creature like me that I should have been half so pleased with as my little Golden Thread. Why, since she came into the world, it isn't the same world it was before, and I ain't the same woman. But I have not been so thankful as I ought. I've grumbled and fretted a good deal because I was so poor.

And yet I'd rather have my little Golden Thread than all the money and all the houses and all the good things there are in the world!"

While these thoughts lighted up the little obscure room in which the poor woman lived, Tangle Thread's mother sat in her beautiful house sad and sorrowful. What to do next for her child she knew not. But God saw her grief and pain, and heard her prayers. He put new courage and patience into her heart. She said to herself: "I have a very hard task to perform. I *must* teach this child obedience. But I see that this cannot be done at once. I must go on day after day, trusting in God to lead me every step of the way. I must pray more, I must love her more, I must be more gentle and tender. But I *must* have her obedience."

Tangle Thread stood, meanwhile, with a dark and gloomy face, near the window. A little bird hung near her in his cage, and she looked at him as he hopped about picking up his seeds, and said, half-aloud:

"I wish *I* was a bird! Then I'd fly away—away off where there are no houses and no people, and where I should have nobody to plague me."

"Poor little unhappy child!" said her mother; "don't you know who it is that 'plagues' you?"

"Everybody does!" cried Tangle Thread. "Papa does, and you do, and Ruth does. You all seem to think I am always naughty."

"Poor child!" repeated her mother, "it is you who torment yourself. But I will not argue with you. I will tell you once more what I have often told you. I cannot treat you exactly as God treats me, for I am a sinful, ignorant creature. I make mistakes, and He never does. I get out of patience, and He does not. I know almost nothing, and He knows everything. But I mean to *try* to treat you, as nearly as I can, as He does me. He has had patience with me a great many times, when I wonder he was willing to wait for me to be penitent. He has been good to me, and given me many, many things. And He has never ceased to put me under the rod since the day I gave myself away to Him. I don't know which to thank Him for most, His goodness or His severity."

Tangle Thread did not perfectly understand all this. But she saw that her mother spoke out of the very depths of her heart. She saw that she was more than ever resolved to make her obedient. And what she did not understand she felt.

She went away sorrowfully to her play-room, and locked herself in. She could not think what made her feel so sad and unhappy. Her books and her toys did not seem to be what she wanted.

"I don't know what I *do* want!" she said to herself; and tears began to roll down her cheeks.

Ah! little Tangle Thread! This is what you want! To have Jesus touch your heart and make it sorry. To kneel down and tell Him how sad and desolate you feel, and to beg Him to make you His own dear child, and to help you to love and obey Him. And then to run and throw yourself at once into your dear mother's arms, hide your head in her bosom, tell her how grieved you are for all your wilful, naughty ways, and how you want to begin now to be like Jesus, and to love and obey Him!

But the child had not yet learned this sweet lesson. She could not bear to be sorry, much less to own she was sorry.

CHAPTER XX.

As nothing more was said to Tangle Thread about her teaching Golden Thread to read, she saw that her mother did not mean to give her that pleasure on account of her behaviour about the purse. Nor was she now invited to go with her mamma to visit poor people as she had often done. To march into sick-rooms laden with baskets of fruit and flowers, her little figure fairly swelling with pride, had been one of her greatest pleasures. There were some good and kindly feelings mingled with her pride; she liked to see a pale face light up with joy on her entrance, and to see how grateful fruit often was to parched lips.

"There's the makings of a good woman in her, bless her heart!" said one of the poor invalids whom she was often taken to see. This woman had lived in her mother's house as cook; she had heard of Tangle Thread's behaviour through the other servants, and knew pretty well what she was.

About this time, Gertrude, Tangle Thread's little friend, came to spend the day with her.

Soon after dinner Gertrude complained of feeling chilly. Ruth, on hearing this, put more coal on the fire, and made Gertrude wear one of Tangle Thread's flannel sacks. But in a few hours she was quite ill. Tangle Thread ran quickly for her mother, who came at once.

"She surely can have eaten nothing at dinner to make her ill?" said she, turning to Ruth.

"No, ma'am. They had nothing but their mutton-chops, potato, and a rice-pudding. No, it was tapioca-pudding to-day."

"Her head and her hands are quite hot," said Tangle Thread.

"What a child you are!" said her mother, smiling. But she looked anxiously at little Gertrude.

"It is snowing, and is very cold," said she. "I hardly like to send Gertrude home in such a storm. Gertrude, darling, would you feel very badly to stay here to-night?"

"I want to go home," said Gertrude. "I want my own mamma to make me get well."

"I will go for your mamma, and if she thinks it best, she will take you home. But if she thinks it would not be safe, then you will stay here, just to-night, won't you?"

"Oh! yes, just as mamma says," replied Gertrude, and she closed her eyes and fell back fast asleep in Ruth's arms. Tangle Thread ran for a shawl, and covered the sleeping child carefully.

"That's right, dear," said her mother.

"Thank you, that's a good child," said Ruth.

It was just at dusk that Gertrude's mother came hurrying up to the nursery. Gertrude awoke, and stretched her arms towards her dear mamma with a sigh of relief. Once in her arms, she expected to be well.

"I dare not touch you yet, dear," said her mother. "I am all covered with snow. Wait till I can shake it off and get dry. Where do you feel sick, darling?"

"I feel better now. My head aches a little, and I am thirsty. And I am tired a little."

"It never would answer to take her home in this storm," said Tangle Thread's mother. "She may be quite relieved by to-morrow, and we might then take her home safely. I will sleep with her myself, and do everything I can for her."

"I don't know; I feel nervous about illness," replied Gertrude's mother, looking anxiously at the child's glowing cheeks. "Since I lost my little Mary, I am frightened at everything. And Gertrude is just one of those little lovely creatures one is always expecting to lose."

"Can't you stay here with Gertrude?" asked Tangle Thread, who had heard every word of this whispered conversation.

"Ah, no—there's the baby to nurse, and where he is, I must be. But I dare not move Gertrude to-night. Perhaps, after all, it's only a fit of indigestion. My darling," said she, now taking the child from Ruth, "you'll do just what dear mamma wishes—I know you will. You'll stay here to night, and early in the morning I'll come with the carriage and take you home. Only just to-night, dear."

"Yes, mamma," said Gertrude. "If you want me to stay, I will."

CHAPTER XXI.

THEY soon had the child undressed and in a warm bed. She fell asleep again, and though her sleep was restless, she complained of nothing when she woke, only once when she tried to take some water, she said: "It hurts me when I drink; I don't want any more water." Her mother, having sat by her side all the evening, was now preparing to go home, and did not hear these words. Tangle Thread's mother did.

"Can her throat be sore?" she said to herself. "Is it possible that scarlet fever has crossed our threshold?" Her heart yearned over her own child. "Oh! if she should have it and die!"

"If there are any alarming symptoms during the night, I had better send for the doctor, had I not?" she said, as Gertrude's mother took leave.

"Certainly, certainly. But I hope she will have a good night, and be quite bright to-morrow."

But the child did not have a good night. She

tossed to and fro and moaned in her sleep, and often said:

"It hurts me where my throat is."

As soon as daylight began to steal into the room, it became plain that Gertrude was covered with an eruption of some sort, and was very ill. The doctor was sent for; he said at once: "Yes, it is scarlet fever!"

"Can I go home to my own mamma?" asked Gertrude.

"We'll send for your mamma to come here," said the doctor. And turning to Tangle Thread's mother, he said:

"As to your own child, you will, of course, see that she does not enter this room."

"But may she not have already taken the disease? She and Gertrude were together all day yesterday."

"I cannot say. We must use the precaution of keeping them apart a couple of weeks, at any rate. As to little Gertrude, if she lives through it, you will have her in this room six weeks."

"If she lives through it! Is she, then, so ill?"

"I think her very ill. And you know what scarlet fever is. But we will do all we can. It is not necessary to alarm her mother. She will take the alarm when she hears what the disease is."

H

Gertrude's mother soon came in, and a glance at her child told her the whole story.

"Nobody need tell me what it is!" she cried, bursting into tears. "It is scarlet fever! O, my little Gertrude! My sweetest, my best child! I never thought she would live to grow up! I knew she was too good! But I never dreamed it would come so soon!"

"Hush!" said Tangle Thread's mother, "she is waking; she will hear you. You must put on a cheerful face when she sees you."

"Oh! how can I look cheerful when my heart is breaking?"

"Come into the next room till you are more composed. And stay yourself on God, my dear friend. He will not touch a hair of Gertrude's head unless it is best. And if it *is* best—if He does take her from you—you will still have Him left. But do not be discouraged. You are not in a state to judge fairly how she is. You look as if you had not slept an hour since you left us last night."

"I did not close my eyes. Something kept saying: 'Gertrude is going just where little Mary did.'"

"Little Mary went to a very happy place!"

"Yes, yes, I know. But oh! she left such a great chasm when she went away. You never lost a child. You don't know anything about it. This world never has seemed the same to me since I lost my little Mary."

"Nor has the next world either. You have often told me how much nearer, how much dearer heaven had been made to you by that affliction. And it will become yet nearer and dearer if your precious little Gertrude goes there too. But God *will not* take her away unless it is best. Let us believe that. Let us trust her to Him. He never makes mistakes, nor snatches away our treasures a moment too soon."

Gertrude's mother dried her tears. "I will trust Him," said she. "I thank Him for giving me such a friend as you to lean on in this time of trouble. But what am I thinking of?" she cried, suddenly. "Here is your child, your only child, exposed to this fearful disease! And I thought only of myself!"

"I must do what I have been urging you to do. I must *trust in God*," replied Tangle Thread's mother.

CHAPTER XXII.

LITTLE GERTRUDE remained very ill many weeks. Her precious life hung, as it were, on a thread. A little self-will on her part, a want of docility in submitting to painful remedies, would have broken that thread at any moment. But she lay, with little meekly-folded hands, on her weary bed, behaving and quieting herself like a weaned child. There was never a frown, nor an impatient word. She let the doctor and her mother and all her friends do what was thought best to do, without in any way resisting their wishes.

Her mother never left her, save now and then to weep in secret.

" She will not get well," said she. " She is too patient, too gentle, too lovely for this world."

Everybody thought as she did. Tangle Thread's mother looked at this little lamb as upon one already chosen of Christ, and precious. She had never seen such sweet submission and docility.

"I never look at her," she whispered to Gertrude's mother, "without thinking of the lines:

> "'Sweet to lie passive in Thy hands,
> And know no will but Thine.'"

"I have learned at last to say those blessed words out of the depths of my own heart," was the answer. "I have no longer any choice about my child. If she is bound heavenward, I will not detain her."

Meanwhile, Tangle Thread's restless, wilful soul was quite subdued by the silence and sadness that reigned in the house. Nothing now would tempt her to indulge in those angry screams that used to resound through every room. She spoke in a low voice, walked softly up and down the stairs, and seemed quite another child. Indeed, her habit of crying aloud with rage was now broken up once for all.

"Do you think Gertrude will get well?" she asked Ruth anxiously, every hour; and Ruth always replied: "Yes, I hope so."

But at last she could not help saying:

"No, I do not. Children like her always die. It is the cross, hateful ones that get well."

"Then, if I am taken sick, I suppose, I shall get well," said Tangle Thread. But after a time she started up, and cried out:

" But *everybody* dies some time or other. Does everybody get good first?"

" I don't know. And I don't know as I did right to say Gertrude wouldn't get well. The doctor says her goodness is in her favour. She takes everything so beautifully, you can't think. And now they're trying to feed her up, and she has to take brandy and beef-tea and all sorts of things so often. And if she was naughty, and would not take them, or if she cried and fretted about them, then she certainly would die."

" But beef-tea is very nice," said Tangle Thread.

" Nice to people that feel pretty well. But Gertrude is so weak that she can hardly swallow. It tires her dreadfully to take anything. Why, I heard of a little boy who starved to death because he would not take the nice, nourishing things he needed. His father got down on his knees, and begged him, with tears in his eyes, to take just a little bit of wine-jelly, and he wouldn't. So he died. It's a very bad thing for a child to be self-willed when it is well; but when it is sick, it is perfectly dreadful."

" I mean to be very good when I am sick," replied Tangle Thread. " I feel a little sick now. I wish you would look down my throat, and see if there's anything the matter with it."

" Oh! there's nothing the matter with your

throat," said Ruth, trying to believe what she said. "Who told you Gertrude's throat was sore?"

"Why, nobody. I didn't know it was sore. But I know mine is. And I know my head aches."

"Dear me! I hope you're not going to be sick!" cried Ruth. "I'm sure your mamma has her hands full now. Well, well, what is to be will have to be. Come here; sit in my lap, and lay your head on my shoulder. Poor little thing! her head *is* hot, I declare."

"Why, Ruth, you seem to love me!" said poor Tangle Thread, bursting into tears.

CHAPTER XXIII.

RUTH could not help crying a little when Tangle Thread said that.

"I'm sure I've always loved you when you were good," she replied. "And you have been a very nice little girl lately. But I suppose I ought to go and tell your mamma that you don't feel well. Only I hate to worry her."

"If I am sick and die, then she won't have anybody to tease her," said Tangle Thread. "And she'll have plenty of time to read and to paint, and everything."

"She'd rather have you than the time," said Ruth. "It would just break her heart if you should die. But don't talk that way. You are not going to die. You are going to get well, and be the best little girl that ever lived. And while you're sick we'll take such good care of you! And when you get well, I'll ask your mamma to let me take you home with me; and you shall drink new milk right from the cow, and you'll grow strong and fat again."

But Tangle Thread had fallen into a heavy sleep, and did not hear Ruth's cheerful words.

Ruth placed her on the bed, covered her with a blanket, and went to tell her mother how ill she seemed. The doctor happened to come in at that moment to see little Gertrude, and he went at once to look at Tangle Thread. There was not much to say or to do. He promised to come in again in a few hours, and then returned to Gertrude.

Tangle Thread's mamma was very quiet, but her heart felt heavy indeed.

" If Tangle Thread should be as ill as Gertrude," she said to Ruth, " she cannot live, she is so very unlike Gertrude."

Ruth made some cheering, pleasant answer, and began to arrange things in the nursery as if she expected Tangle Thread to remain there during her illness.

" Oh! I shall have Tangle Thread in my room," said her mother.

" I was hoping to keep her here, ma'am," said Ruth. " I'll take the very best care of her. And you are worn out now with little Gertrude's sickness, and so many coming and going."

" Thank you, Ruth. You are very kind, but I

feel that I must have Tangle Thread in my own room. You must remember she is all I have." And then the thought that she might now be about to lose that all, made her eyes fill with tears, and she sat down by the bed, and hid her face in her child's pillow, and silently wept and prayed.

Tangle Thread awoke and started up, looking flushed and distressed.

" O mamma! is Gertrude dead?" she cried.

" No, my darling; Gertrude seems a little better to-day."

" Then what makes you cry so?"

" Oh! I am not crying much," replied her mother. " I suppose I am pretty tired with watching Gertrude; and so when I heard you were sick, too, I could not help shedding a few tears. You see mamma loves you very much, and it grieves her to see you suffer. But now you are going into my room to sleep with me in my bed, and I shall take care of you day and night. And if you will try to be patient and docile, like Gertrude, you will get well before long."

" I will try," replied Tangle Thread.

She was very glad to be undressed and to lay her head on the cool pillow in her mamma's own bed. She passed a weary night, and only slept in snatches.

When the doctor came the next day, he knew, and they all knew, that she had the fever with which Gertrude had been so ill.

And now the fruits of her mamma's long patience showed themselves. Tangle Thread did not submit to painful remedies as sweetly as Gertrude had done ; and sometimes she cried, and was peevish and unreasonable. But she had been learning lessons of obedience all her life, and now she was humbled and subdued by greater suffering than she had ever known. So she never absolutely resisted the doctor's wishes nor her mamma's. She was not so ill as Gertrude had been, but she had a long and tedious sickness, and passed many weary hours. Her mamma seldom left her, and did all she could to make her forget her sufferings.

After a time, little Gertrude, whose room was on the same floor, was brought, in the nurse's arms, to make Tangle Thread a visit. The poor little creature was very feeble. She could not hold up her head, nor could she amuse herself in any way.

" Why don't you tell Gertrude stories, mamma, and sing to her ?" asked Tangle Thread.

" The poor little thing cannot hear," replied her mamma. " It makes my heart ache when I see how little we can any of us do for her."

"Why can't she hear?" asked Tangle Thread, in surprise. "She used to hear as well as I did."

"Yes, but she has been very, very ill. And it will be a long time before she can hear stories, if ever."

"I will give her all my toys, then," said Tangle Thread. "My Paris doll and all its clothes; its dotted muslin frock and its pink silk, and its gaiter-boots, and its bracelets, and its watch, and its pocket-handkerchief and under-sleeves and collars."

"But Gertrude has a little Eugénie already."

"So she has—I forgot it." And so saying, Tangle Thread buried her face in the pillow and began to cry pitifully.

Her mamma was afraid she would make herself very ill by crying so. She told Gertrude's nurse to take her away; and then leaning over the bed, she said gently, but very firmly:

"You must stop crying, my child."

"I can't," sobbed Tangle Thread, "I'm *so* tired! And I don't want Gertrude not to hear."

"I am sorry I let you know that," said her mamma, kissing her, and stroking back the hair that had fallen over her face. "But now **stop** crying; for I have two things to say to you, and you can't hear unless you are quiet."

Tangle Thread stopped crying, and wiped her eyes.

"You must not break your heart about little Gertrude," said her mother. "The doctor hopes, and we all hope, that by-and-by her hearing will return to her. But if it never does, her dear Saviour, who loves her so, and who has been with her all through her sickness, will comfort her and make her happy. Even at the longest, we do not stay in this world very long. Little Gertrude will only have to be patient a few years, and then God will take her to heaven, where she will hear just as well as you and I. You know we mustn't be always thinking how we are to get along with the troubles we have in this world. We must be thinking how sweet heaven will be when we get there."

Tangle Thread's face began to look a little brighter. But after a moment she said:

"But Gertrude's mamma will feel so sorry!"

"Yes, she feels very sorry already. But then Gertrude's mamma loves Jesus dearly. And she likes to have Him do just what He thinks best."

"But what makes Him think it best to make people deaf?"

"I do not know. I do not expect to understand everything He does. When the doctor used such painful remedies for your throat, you did not expect to understand why he used them. You let him do what he pleased, because you knew he was wise and kind."

Tangle Thread smiled. After a time she said:

"What was the other thing you were going to say, mamma?"

"I was going to say that, on the whole, you have been very good while you were ill. I expected to have a hard time with you. I thought you would be unwilling to take your medicines and to do other things the doctor desired. But we have had some quite happy hours together since you were moved into this room. So you are not to be called Tangle Thread any longer. You are to be called my little Silver Thread."

"That's nice! that's *real* nice! But, O mamma! what has become of Golden Thread?"

"She has not been here during your illness, I believe. I must send some one to see how they are. And, my darling, don't you think that before long you will become a little Golden Thread?"

"I don't know. I'm afraid I never shall be so good as that," replied Silver Thread, whose ideas on the subject had undergone a great change since the time when she said: "I can be whatever I please!"

"You are to be called my little Silver Thread."—P. 110.

CHAPTER XXIV.

During Gertrude's illness and Tangle Thread's, nobody had had much time to think of Golden Thread. For four weeks Gertrude's mother had never undressed, and the whole house had been full of care and anxiety. But now both children were out of danger, and Ruth was very glad to run around as before among the poor and the sick. She was particularly glad to be sent to inquire after Golden Thread and her mother, for she liked them both. And they liked her, and were thankful to see her pleasant face once more. At least, Golden Thread was. As to her poor mother, her eyes were worse than ever, so that she could not use them at all, and she looked pale and thin. She said the doctor had told her she never would get well while she lived in that house; there was water in the cellar, and the whole street was damp and unwholesome. She felt discouraged and anxious, and thought she never should be able to see again. But she still had great comfort in her good, loving child, and said the world could not seem quite dark to her while Golden Thread was in it, happen what might.

"It comes very hard on poor folks to be sick," said she. "It is many a long day since I earned a penny, and my strength seems all gone."

Then Ruth told her all about the two sick children at their house; how lovely little Gertrude had been, and how she had lain nine days so ill that they thought she might die at any moment. And how Tangle Thread's name had been changed to Silver Thread, because she had behaved so much better during her sickness than ever before in her life.

"You see rich folks have their troubles as well as poor folks," added Ruth. "And our folks make a good use of theirs. It seemed as if they were as kind to the poor and the sick as they well could be, but they're even kinder now. Why, when I go home and tell how you're getting on, and what the doctor says, I'm sure they'll be for moving you into a healthier place."

"But rents are higher in better houses," returned the poor woman.

"Of course. And our notions about goodness have risen a peg or two higher," said Ruth, laughing. "I've been thinking it over since I came in, and I've made up my mind to let you have so much a month out of my wages. I get good wages, and many a present besides. If you ever get well you can pay me again, you know."

Ruth did not really expect this poor blind woman to be able to repay her. She only said this to comfort her. She went home quite pleased and happy; but there she found dismal news awaiting her. Her mother had written to say that all sorts of trouble had come upon them. The big barn had burned down, and one of the horses was lame, and "father" had the rheumatism, and some of their best milk and butter customers had fallen off. Poor Ruth had a good cry, and sat up late that night writing a long letter in reply. She said there should be another big barn built out of her savings; she was going to be very careful and not waste a penny; then the horse would certainly get well in time for the spring work, and she knew father's rheumatism would go off when warm weather came, especially if he would use the liniment she was going to send him. And as to the milk and butter, why, if folks wouldn't buy it, suppose they got somebody to come and eat and drink it? That is, suppose they took in one or two boarders this coming summer? And just as she said that, a thought came into her head that made her get up and look at herself in the

I

glass, to see what sort of a body it was that could make such splendid plans.

" Mother would like the company, and she wouldn't have to put herself out at all for them. There's plenty of house-room, and plenty to eat and drink. If they once went there, they'd be likely to stay year in and year out. And Golden Thread is a good, handy child; she'd soon save mother some steps. Mother would get fond of her, I know. Let me see; what was it I promised to give them? I do believe I said I would pay the difference in their rent, if they'd move. But, of course, I can't do that, and let my own father suffer. Well, I won't worry about it. It will all come out right in the end—I'm sure it will ! "

CHAPTER XXV.

On hearing Ruth's account of the state in which she had found the poor blind woman—for she was now really quite blind—Silver Thread was full of pity.

"Do go to see her, mamma," said she. "And do carry lots of things to her."

Her mamma sat silent and thoughtful, and did not seem to hear.

"Mamma! *mamma!*" repeated Silver Thread, impatiently.

The mother was still silent.

"You won't do a thing I want you to," said Silver Thread, rudely.

Her mamma started. "I was trying to think what I could do for that poor woman," she answered. "And I did not think my little Silver Thread would ever speak to me in that way again."

"I don't know how I came to do it," said Silver Thread, sorrowfully.

Oh! how quickly these few words, this gentle tone, set everything right between them!

But Silver Thread was very feeble, and she now began to cry bitterly.

"Don't cry, my darling," said her mamma. "I ought not to expect you to cure yourself of your bad habits at once. But now let me tell you what I have been planning. I will go to see Dr. A., and find out just what he thinks of this poor woman. He certainly seemed to think he could cure her eyes when I took her to him. But if he says he cannot, then I think a nice, quiet home in the country somewhere, would be better for her general health than the best home in the city."

"Yes, my general health is better in the country," said Silver Thread, wiping her eyes. "And Golden Thread would like to go, I know. Do please, mamma, order the carriage and see about it at once. Ruth can come and tell me stories while you are gone."

"I thought Ruth was not gifted in story-telling."

"Well, it isn't stories exactly. It's talk. She talks about her father's farm, and the horses, chickens, and such things."

"Her father's farm? Why, that would be such a very nice place for our poor blind woman! Ruth's mother is one of the kindest creatures in the world. I wonder if she would mind the care? I could make it quite an object to her."

Ruth came in now to say that the carriage was ready, and Silver Thread was glad when she heard her mamma drive off in it.

"Only to think, Ruth!" said she; "mamma has gone to see the doctor about Golden Thread's mother. She is going to ask him if he thinks it would be good for her to go into the country to live. And she says she wonders if your mother would let her come there, because she could make it quite an object to her."

"Well! if I ever!" cried Ruth. "If the very same idea didn't come into my head! Only I didn't mean to have your mother pay a penny. I expected to manage it, somehow, myself."

"It will be splendid!" said Silver Thread.

They chatted on awhile, until the clock struck.

"It's time for you to take your beef-tea," said Ruth. "Do you mind staying alone while I run down for it?"

"Oh! I don't believe it is time yet," replied Silver Thread. "You can't think how I hate it. I don't see what the doctor makes me take it for."

"You said once that beef-tea was very nice. And you know you must take it, whether or no."

Silver Thread began to fret and to mutter.

"Won't let me have any peace. Keep pouring

down the beef-tea, and pouring it down. Won't
let me go to sleep, or anything. Say it's four
o'clock when it isn't four o'clock. Do all they can
to plague me."

She spent the time of Ruth's absence in this
state of ill-humour, and swallowed her beef-tea
with grimaces. How many half-starved children
would have been thankful for every drop!

Ruth quieted and soothed Silver Thread, and
made all sorts of excuses for her.

"You are weak and tired," said she. "Perhaps I let you talk too much. Now lie down and
I'll sing to you. Poor little Gertrude can't hear
singing or talking, and you can. Now shut your
eyes and lie still, and perhaps you'll get a little
nap, and then you'll wake up just in time to hear
what your mamma has to say."

Silver Thread was very tired—too tired to fret
any more. She lay still and soon fell asleep, and
when she awoke her mamma had come home.

"How have you been, my darling?" she asked,
sitting down by the bed.

"Rather cross," said Silver Thread.

Her mamma smiled, not expecting just such an
answer.

"Well, let me tell you what Dr. A. says. I
found him at home, and he was very glad to see
me. He says the poor creature's eyes are past

cure. She was a good deal worn-out with hard work when the accident happened, and then she has been living in such an unwholesome place. Otherwise he might, perhaps, have saved her eyes."

" And she went to a quack doctor first," said Silver Thread.

" Yes, that was another thing. So now, if she likes the plan, we'll get her into the country very soon."

" Ruth says her mother will let her come there, she is almost sure."

" That will be very pleasant. Ruth could go with them and arrange everything. Ruth needs a little change. I thought this morning she did not look well."

" Oh! that is because her father's barn got burned down, and ever so many other things happened."

It was too late to do anything more that night. But Silver Thread went to sleep in good spirits, with a great deal that was pleasant to think of. She dreamed that she saw Golden Thread running about in the fields gathering buttercups, and as bright and happy as a bird. She saw her drinking fresh milk, and growing fat on it. She thought she heard her say: " Oh! how glad I am I came here! I never want to go and live in a big city again, as long as I live."

CHAPTER XXVI.

FROM being a very unhappy child, Silver Thread was becoming a happy one. Do you know the reason? It was because God has so made us, that while we spend our time in thinking of nobody's comfort but our own, the best things in the world fail to please us. A child may have all the beautiful toys it wants, and a pleasant home and the kindest friends, and yet be restless, peevish, and uncomfortable. But when it begins to try to be gentle and patient with everybody; when it speaks pleasant words and gives up its own way, then a black cloud seems to clear away from before its eyes, and it walks on in sunshine. Poor Silver Thread had spent her whole life in troubling and grieving her dear mother, and her nurse, and all about her; but she did not know it was that which made her often go away by herself to be sullen and sad in secret, nor did she now quite understand what it was that made her, lying there so feeble on her sick-bed, have so many hours of sweet peace.

Now, if you want to understand what I have been saying better, let us suppose you get up to-morrow morning, and begin the day by fretting all the time your nurse, or your mamma, or your sister, is washing and dressing you. You can cry when your hair is combed, and say she hurts you. You can pull away from her while she is putting on your clothes. Then, when you go down to breakfast, you can find fault with it, or get vexed because you can't eat more than is good for you. After breakfast, if you have lessons to learn, you can cry again over them, and soil your book, and annoy every one in the room. Then, if your mamma wishes you to go out to walk, you can dispute with her about what you shall wear. You can be very disagreeable if she says you are to wear your over-shoes, and declare that it is quite dry out of doors. After you get home, you can take your little bro-ther's chair, and when he cries for it—for why shouldn't he cry, if you do?—you can call him a cry-baby, and tell him to take his old chair, in a very unpleasant way. If any of the other children ask you to lend them your knife or your pencil, you can say: "What plagues you are! Why didn't you tell me you wanted it before I sat down? And if I lend you my pencil you'll break off the point, and then I shall have to keep stopping to cut it."

When it comes night, and you are told it is time to go to bed, you can say: " O dear! *must* I go to bed? Can't I sit up a little longer? I don't believe it is eight o'clock." When, at last, those you have teased and annoyed all day get you off to bed, they feel relieved, and as if they should now have a little peace. And you lie down on your pillow, dissatisfied, out of sorts, and ready to get up next morning peevish and tiresome.

But let us suppose just the contrary. You get up pleasant, and if your little sister is going to be dressed first, you wait patiently for your turn. If your nurse pulls your hair when she combs it, you can tell her so, gently, and ask her to please to be more careful. You can go down stairs smiling and pleasant, and ready to say good morning cheerfully to everybody. If your mamma says you are to have less breakfast than usual, because you had headache yesterday, you will not say a word, but eat what she gives you, and be thankful it is so much. If she wants you to amuse the baby while she washes the silver or breakfast-cups, you won't answer, " Oh! I was just going out to play," but will give her a sweet smile and a sweet word. If one of the other children gets your toy, you will not run to snatch it away; you will say, " Please,

Mary, give me my doll;" and having always seen your good example, she will be likely to give it up without a word. If you are busy reading, you will lay aside your book pleasantly when your papa asks you to run to get the paper for him, and he will kiss you and be thankful he has such a little girl when you come tripping back with it. You will lie down to sleep at night, peaceful and happy, knowing that you have tried all day long to do right, and to do it in a pleasant way.

Now, Silver Thread could not turn all at once into such ways as these. Every now and then her old, naughty habits would come like armed men, and seem to *make* her do and say things she did not want to say. Then she would be quite provoked with herself, and think there was no use in trying. And sometimes, after praying to God to make her good, she felt impatient with Him for not making her perfect without giving her the trouble of trying to be so. But there's no use in being discouraged. It is better for a poor naughty child that *wants* to do right, but finds it very hard, to keep right on trying and trying, and praying and praying, hoping on, and hoping ever.

But perhaps you think this sort of talk is too much like a sermon, and at any rate we had better see what Golden Thread and her mother have to say about going into the country. You must re-

member that except her own sweet temper, Golden
Thread had not much in this world.   She was not
yet old enough to do any sort of work that would
help much toward the support of her mother, and
yet her head was quite full of plans as to what she
would do as soon as she grew taller and stronger.
She thought she could go and live somewhere as
little maid, and so earn a trifle—enough to get a
room in a house where the cellar was not damp;
and though it made the tears come into her eyes
to think of it, she was resolved to do so very soon.
Her mother knew it would have to come to that
sooner or later, but it almost broke her heart to
think of being left alone and blind, without her
bright Golden Thread's cheery words and ways.
Ruth's visits comforted them both for a time, but
then the poor mother grew sad again.

"If we are going to live on charity," said she,
"we may as well go to the workhouse first as last.
And I don't see much chance of our living on
anything else."

"But if we could get along a little while longer,
mother, just till I grow a bit taller, I could get a
place, and then you wouldn't have to live on charity."

"It will be many a long year before you could
earn money. Nobody would give you more than
your board and clothes."

"But that would be a good deal. And I would try to do everything I could to please them. Don't cry, dear mother."

"I can't help crying; when I think that ever since I was eight years old I've earned my own bread, and no thanks to anybody; and now I'm helpless, and have to demean myself to be a beggar!"

"Why, mother! are you a *beggar?*" cried Golden Thread.

"It's just the same. I eat other people's bread, and wear other people's clothes, and use other people's money. And I can't do a thing for them that feed and clothe me."

"Can't you pray for them, mother? Praying's *something.*"

The poor woman was silent. What little praying she had ever done in her life had been for herself, in her misery, and for her child.

"Such prayers as mine wouldn't do them any good," she said at last.

"Well, maybe they'll do a little bit of good," urged Golden Thread. "I pray for that kind lady every night. And for that little girl, too. My teacher said we ought to pray for everybody that is kind to us."

"What do you say?"

"I say: 'Our Father who art in heaven!'"

"What, the Lord's Prayer? I don't call that praying for the lady, or the little girl either."

"Isn't it?" said Golden Thread, greatly disappointed and puzzled. "Why, I meant it, all the same. I don't know anything else to say, and so whenever I think of them, and how good the lady was, I say, 'Our Father.' Maybe He knows what I mean."

The poor woman sighed. "Ah! my child knows more than I do, and is better, too," thought she. "I've never taught her anything good, and now she's teaching me. I'm afraid I ain't just what I ought to be; but I don't know. I never wronged anybody in my life, nor told a lie, nor took a pin that wasn't mine. But I can't say what's wanting in me."

CHAPTER XXVII.

"Do you think, Ruth, that this poor blind woman and her child would give your mother too much trouble?" asked Silver Thread's mamma. "You know I owe them a heavy debt of gratitude, and I am resolved to place them in some pleasant country place, where the child can be learning to do such kinds of work as she is capable of, and where the mother can recruit."

"I think my mother would be very glad to take them, ma'am," replied Ruth. "Golden Thread is such a nice, pleasant child, and her mother is so grateful and humble."

"I don't know about the humility," said Silver Thread's mother, smiling a little. "But I think well of her, and the child has fairly won my heart."

"The only trouble is, to get the poor creature to consent to go at your expense, ma'am. It almost kills her to live on charity."

"Did Elijah live on charity when the ravens fed him?" asked Silver Thread, in her wise little way.

"I shouldn't think it was charity; I should think it was God," she added. "Besides, Golden Thread saved my life, and mamma would want to give her lots of things for that. Oh! you needn't laugh, Ruth. She really did save my life! There were all the coaches and carts and carriages going up and down, and I might have been run over. And she risked her life for me."

"Yes, yes," said her mother. "I do really owe them far more than I can ever repay. But this is nothing to the debt I owe my heavenly Father, and He intends that those of His children to whom he has given money shall use it for Him. I am only thankful that He has thrown this poor woman in my way. And now, how very nice it will be, if we can put her under your mother's care! Do write to her by this evening's mail, and see what she will say. Or stay—suppose you run down and see her, and talk with her about it? You can take the seven o'clock train to-morrow morning, and come back by the early train the day after. Then if we decide to send Golden Thread and her mother, you can go with them, and stay a few days until they feel at home."

Ruth felt very grateful for this proposal, and at

twelve o'clock next day she ate dinner with her father and mother, to their no small delight. Everything was easily arranged. There was a room that could be spared as well as not; it was warmed in winter by a remarkable stove funnel that ran through it without heating it at all in summer; there was a pleasant prospect from the window, of a strip of white sanded beach and blue waters beyond, and of green trees and meadows between.

"To be sure, if the poor creature is blind, the prospect does not so much matter," said Ruth's mother; "but then the little girl can tell her about it, and not let her think I put her to sleep with her face to the barn. And you say it is a nice child? I always did say a little girl round the house was a nuisance I couldn't and wouldn't bear; but then some little girls ain't like all little girls."

"This one is the nicest child I ever saw," returned Ruth. "And you'll teach her your own ways, mother, won't you? She is not to be brought up a fine lady—that I was to make sure of; but to be an industrious girl, able to do all sorts of work. Why, she'll save you some steps, now, mother."

"She won't save as many as she'll make," replied the mother, whose opinion of "little girls"

K

was not flattering. " But you may depend I'll do my best for her and her poor mother too."

Ruth went back to town quite relieved of all anxiety.

"O mamma!" cried Silver Thread eagerly, "let me tell Golden Thread she is to go to the country. She will be so glad!　Mayn't I tell her?"

" I don't know, darling.　I am not quite sure that Golden Thread ought to be exposed to take the fever by coming here.　On the whole, I do not think it would be safe."

" It's too bad!" cried Silver Thread.

" Is anything God does 'too bad'?" asked her mother, gently.　"You know it was He who sent you sickness, and it is He who makes it unsafe for children to come to see you."

" I didn't think," said Silver Thread.　" But I should like so much to tell Golden Thread."

" Very likely you would be disappointed, if you could see and tell her.　She knows nothing about the country, and cannot go into ecstasies at the thought of living in it.　I will tell you all she does say when I come home, for I am going now to see them.　Perhaps they will prefer to stay in town.　In that case, of course I cannot force them to leave it."

At first it did seem as if leaving the noisy, dirty, unwholesome city was going to be a trial, instead of a blessing. The poor woman was so feeble that the thought of exerting herself to make any change made her begin to cry. Then Golden Thread cried too, and things looked forlorn.

"It's so hard to go among strangers," said the woman. "And to live on charity! If I could do anything to pay my way, it would be so different! But I never lived on charity till now."

One needs patience with poor people as well as with little children. Silver Thread's mother had to try hard not to lose hers, now.

"While you were well and strong," said she, "it was quite right for you to work, and not to accept charity. But now God has laid His hand on you, and set you aside from labour of any kind. And seeing you so helpless, He has sent me to do for you what you can't do for yourself."

"I never thought as God had anything to do with it. It was the whitewash and the bad doctoring, and the damp room and all, that broke me down. I don't mean any harm. I am a poor ignorant creature, and can't reason things out very well. But the workhouse is good enough for such as we are; and we'd better go there, if we must go anywhere."

"Golden Thread, did you ever see any pretty white hens?" asked the lady. "Ruth says her mother's hens are all pure white, every one of them. And they have cows, too—I don't know how many; and when she was a little girl, she used to drive them home from pasture every evening. You would like to feed the hens and chickens, I'm sure. And you can't think how sweet and still it is in the country. Very soon the spring will open, then the fields will be green and covered with flowers; the birds will begin to sing and to build their nests, and everything will be bright and beautiful. Then as the summer comes on, you will go out to pick berries in the fields and woods. And you will be learning all sorts of things. You will learn to milk and to hunt for eggs, and by-and-by to make butter and cheese."

Golden Thread smiled. She began to think the country must be nice, after all. To make butter and cheese! Why, that must be better than living in the city! But then, she did not want to do anything mother didn't, and mother kept crying!

"My little daughter wanted very much to break this good news to you," added the lady, smiling. "But I thought it very likely it wouldn't seem good news at first. It is not necessary to decide what you will do at once. You can think it over, and pray it over; and by-and-by you will see just what is best to do."

"Shall we say anything besides 'Our Father?'"

asked Golden Thread. "I don't know any prayer but that, and I don't think mother does."

"I would say that, and I would, besides, tell God just how troubled and perplexed you feel. Tell Him you do not know whether to stay here or go into the country. Ask Him to make you do whatever is best and will please Him most." She spoke to the child, but she hoped the mother would lay her words to heart.

"Now good-bye," she added, rising to go. "Don't feel troubled and unhappy. You will see your way out of this strait, I have no doubt." She shook hands with them both, and took leave.

CHAPTER XXVIII.

On hearing the result of her mamma's visit, Sil-ver Thread was quite vexed with Golden Thread and her mother.

"They are not nice people at all," said she. "They are ungrateful. I hope you never will give them anything again, mamma."

"It is fortunate that the affairs of this world are not in the hands of ignorant little children," replied her mamma, smiling. "So you would have me turn my back upon them because they do not jump at my offer?"

"That's what they deserve."

"But what do you and I deserve? Suppose God should give us exactly what we deserve, what would He give us, do you think? O, my darling! what a mercy it is that He does not! And we must try to be long-suffering and patient, as He is, and not be harsh with our fellow-creatures."

Silver Thread was silent. She was glad, when Ruth come in, to see the colour rush into her

cheeks when told that the poor woman did not
entirely fancy the idea of going to live in the
country.

"It's only too good for such as her to be offered
the privilege of going to live with such as my
mother!" she said, quickly. "I begin to see now
that you were right, ma'am, in saying she was as
proud as she could be."

"I am not aware that I said that, Ruth. You
forget yourself. I barely suggested that she had
less humility than you fancied; and that rather
to prepare you for the disappointment I thought
might await you. As to pride, we all have it in
one shape or other."

"It's a very ugly shape when it makes a body
so stuck up," said Ruth, who rarely lost her temper, but when she did, hardly knew where to look
for it.

"I never saw it in any shape but an ugly one,"
was the answer. "It is certainly very unpleasant
to see people too proud to receive favours. But
it is also unpleasant to see people too proud of
their own virtues to make allowances for the faults
of others."

Ruth coloured.

"I do not mean to be severe with you, Ruth.
We are none of us guiltless in this respect. And
do not feel irritated about this matter. The next

time you see that poor woman, she will, as likely as not, have changed her mind."

It turned out to be exactly so. The poor woman was beginning to feel the effects of God's Spirit on her heart. She tried to pray as she had been urged to do, and Golden Thread prayed too, that they might be led to do what would please Him. They were groping their way toward Him in the dark, as it were, and He was coming to meet them more than half-way, as our gracious Lord always does to those who seek Him.

"Mother," said Golden Thread, "is it nice in the country?"

"Folks say it is. I've always thought it must be lonesome. Now here you see the carriages going up and down, and crowds of people stirring about, and everybody so wide awake."

"But you can't see them now, mother."

"No, that's true enough. And the noise in my ears does tire me some days. Maybe, too, you'd take a liking to the country yourself."

"I should if you did," replied Golden Thread.

The next day, Ruth, a little ashamed of her anger, asked leave to go and carry Golden Thread a few fresh eggs which she had brought for her from the farm.

The child and her mother were delighted. A breeze from the farmhouse seemed to come invitingly to meet them. That unknown land, "the country," did not seem so strange since it sent those white eggs.

"Don't you think your mother will wish we hadn't come, after she's had us a little while?" asked the woman. "For we shall be a sight of trouble."

"No, you won't," answered Ruth. "Golden Thread can take all the care of you, lead you about, and all that, and by degrees you will grow stronger, and can help more than you'll hinder. And Golden Thread will wash dishes and set the table and feed the hens and chickens. There's my little block that I used to stand on when I wasn't high enough to reach up to the sink; there's my piece of tin on it now that I nailed on one end of it."

"What was the tin for?" asked Golden Thread.

"Why, my block was going to split, and I nailed on a bit of tin to keep it together."

"Isn't it lonesome in the country?" asked the poor woman, a little timidly.

"I don't think it's lonesome anywhere where my mother is," said Ruth. "But then she ain't your mother, and I ought not to expect you to feel as if she was."

"How nice it must be to hunt for eggs!" cried Golden Thread. "And you said we should have as much milk as we wanted! It doesn't seem as if there was as much milk in the world as that!"

They all laughed, and Golden Thread's mother began to think how pleasant it would be for the child to leave that dirty street and breathe the pure country air. She began to wonder how she had happened to think so much of herself, and so little of that good patient child whom she had never yet heard speak one unkind word.

"O Ruth! if your mother will let us, we'll go!" said she; "and we'll try to be as little trouble as we can."

Ruth went away, well satisfied with this sudden change. It was then agreed that on the first of May she should take them to their new home. Meanwhile, dear little Gertrude was slowly regaining her strength, and she and Silver Thread spent many happy hours together with their dolls and other toys.

Silver Thread began to feel as if she had a sweet little sister of her own; and when she, at last, heard that Gertrude was going home, she nearly made herself ill again with crying. Poor little Gertrude could not guess what this terrible distress was about, for they could not make her understand that she was going away. But she tried to comfort Silver Thread with kisses and caresses, and after she had gone everybody tried

to divert the poor broken-hearted child. Her
mamma was very gentle and tender with her, and
talked to her about Jesus, who never has to go
away and leave us, happen what will. And she
let her spend the money in her little purse in
buying some things for Golden Thread's journey.
Silver Thread felt very grateful for this favour,
because this was the very money about which she
had been so naughty. She made up her mind how
she would have it spent, and Ruth went out to get
the things; which were odd enough, you may depend. First, there was a basket to put eggs in,
if she should be so happy as to find any eggs.
Next, there was a small tin cup which she was to
fill with milk, and drink, as soon as she had learned
how to milk all herself. Thirdly, there was a sun-
bonnet which Golden Thread was to wear always
except on Sundays. Fourthly, a penny churn, with
which to make butter. Fifthly, some beans and
peas, which were to be planted in whatever little
corner might be allowed her for a garden. Last
of all, two buns, lest she should be hungry on the
journey. These things being all spread out on her
bed, she looked at them with great satisfaction,
and couldn't help wishing she was going on a
journey, too.

Golden Thread and her mother needed a good
many other things, which were supplied them, and

at last they set off with Ruth, in pretty good spirits. Indeed, Golden Thread would have been as gay as a lark if her mother had not looked so pale and tired; and very soon her amusement and astonishment at everything she saw on the road quite amused and astonished the poor woman herself, and made her glad that her child could be so free from care.

Ruth felt quite proud when she at last ushered its new guests into the neat and cheerful farm-house, and saw how they enjoyed her mother's bread-and-butter, and how her mother enjoyed being kind and friendly to them. After dinner she made the poor tired woman lie down on her bed, when, soothed by the sweet stillness, she soon fell asleep. And then she and Golden Thread went all about the farm, laughing and talking and making merry together with the eggs they found and the eggs they couldn't find, and feeding the hens and paying visits to the cows. Golden Thread lived as much in that one day as she had lived before in a month. Oh! how pleasant everything looked to her! Only she was almost afraid this was only a beautiful dream, and that by-and-by she should wake up and hear the carts go rumbling by, the milkman shrieking, and the neighbours' children quarrelling on the stairs.

CHAPTER XXIX.

RUTH stayed at home four days. She showed
Golden Thread how to do what work she was able
to do, and set up a blue yarn stocking for her
mother to knit, so that she might not be unhappy
from idleness. When she went back to town, she
left them in good spirits, and quite weaned from
the city, which they thought they never should
want to see again. The day after she left was
Sunday, and the farmer brought a waggon to the
door, with two seats, and took them all to church.
It was many a year since the blind woman had
been to the house of God. She used to think
Sunday was only fit to rest in, especially for poor
folks who worked hard all the week. But now
she could not make that excuse, for she was rest-
ing all the week, not working. Nor could she say
her clothes were not decent, for they were as neat
and tidy as clothes could be. So she and Golden
Thread sat together in the farmer's big, square
pew, and had a truly blessed Sunday there. After

church, Ruth's father made Golden Thread stand
by his side and learn the First Commandment, and
spell out a few verses in his big Bible, just as he
used to do years before with Ruth herself. Indeed,
he soon began to treat the child as if she were his
own little Golden Thread, and to love her dearly;
and he and his wife kept saying how nice it was
to have such a cheerful, pleasant little thing about
the house. This did her mother as much good as
the country air and country food did. She began
to feel that they were not a burden, and to recover
her health and spirits. Every pleasant day she
sat with her knitting before the door of the house,
looking as peaceful and happy as if she had never
known a care. Yes, happier and more peaceful,
for God had blessed to her the troubles she had
passed through, and had taught her to love Himself. By degrees she left off complaining that she
never expected to live on charity, and grew humble and thankful, and willing to live just as God
would have her. And after a time she stopped
talking about the loss of her eyes, and only kept
saying how happy she was, in having such a home,
and such friends, and such a child. This made
everybody kind to her; and Ruth's mother, as she
bustled about her work, often looked with envy at
the pale, placid face, and said to herself:

"I'm afraid she's on the way to a great deal

better place than this! But it is a pleasure to do what little one can for her, and to try to make her last days her best days. And if she's going to heaven, I'm glad she took us in her way!"

About two months after Golden Thread's entrance into her new home, she and Silver Thread had the pleasure of meeting again. The doctor wished Silver Thread to travel about a little this summer, and try change of air, because she did not grow very strong, or recover her rosy cheeks. So, for one thing, they all came to this pretty little village; and when Silver Thread came out to the farm, Golden Thread led her about, and showed her all its wonders, and they played together in the hay, and fed the chickens, to their heart's content.

Silver Thread liked being at the farm better than she did staying at the village, when she had no playmate. Her mamma allowed Ruth to take her home to spend a week there, thinking that she would spend more time out of doors, and gain strength faster. This was a very pleasant week to both the children, and they were sorry when Saturday came, and it was time for Silver Thread to go back.

" I've a good mind not to go," she said to Ruth. " I like to stay here, and I think this place agrees with me very well, indeed. Why can't you go to the village and tell mamma I want to stay another week?"

"I should not dare to go without you," replied Ruth. "If your mamma should not choose to have you stay, it would then be too late to take you home to-night. I would go, if I were you, and perhaps she will let you come back next Monday."

"But I want to be here on Sunday. Golden Thread says it is such fun to ride to church in a waggon, and I never rode in a waggon."

"But I am to drive you home in the waggon as soon as we have done supper."

Silver Thread became sullen and silent.

"I don't want to stay where I am not wanted," she said at last.

"We do want you," cried Ruth. "We all want you. But how dare I disobey your mamma? Come! do be good. And I dare say she will let you spend another week."

Silver Thread's old, bad habits were too strong for her. She began to cry in a very disagreeable way, kicking her chair with her feet, and rocking backwards and forwards as if in great distress. Nobody could do anything with her. Golden Thread was frightened, and went and hid in the hay-mow. Supper was ready, but neither of the children ate any. Golden Thread was too unhappy, and Silver Thread was too angry. Ruth's father brought the waggon to the door, lifted the crying child into it, and they drove away. Ruth was thankful to get off; she was ashamed to have her father and mother see such behaviour. By degrees Silver Thread stopped crying. Then she began to feel wofully ashamed. What *had* she been doing? What must they all think? And what would God do with such a child? Ruth drove on in silence. She had felt much vexed with Silver Thread, but she now began to pity her.

"Poor thing!" thought she, "she's got a hard time before her with that temper of hers. She's the very oddest child I ever saw. You never can tell one minute what humour she'll be in the next."

After a time, touched by Silver Thread's swollen, tearful face, and something unusual in its expression, she said:

"Never mind. It's all over now. You needn't be afraid I shall tell your mamma of you."

"I shall tell her myself," was the answer; and then they drove on without another word, till they reached the house where Silver Thread's mamma was living. Ruth was to go home with the waggon, and after lifting the child out, she hastened away, not caring to see the meeting between them.

"Here is your old Tangle Thread come back," said the poor little girl, as her mother ran joyfully to meet her. "I'm not Silver Thread any more. I am worse than cannibals and worse than heathens. I'm perfectly dreadful!"

L

"Why, my dear child, what can you mean?" cried her mother. "What dreadful thing have you been doing? Don't go off and sit by yourself in that way. Come, sit in your own mamma's lap, and tell me all about it. Don't you know how dearly I love you, and how lonely I have been without you?" She took the child in her lap and soothed her tenderly. After a time Silver Thread told the whole story.

"But, my dear little girl, do you expect to become quite good all at once, like a flash of lightning, for instance?"

"I don't know. I know I'm old Tangle Thread, only worse."

Her mamma could not help smiling. "Old Tangle Thread, as you call her," she answered, "has gone away for ever. She has left some of her bad habits behind her, it is true, and they will be often trying to you and to me. Why, 'old Tangle Thread' was not only naughty, but she never tried to be good. This little Silver Thread does try, and that very hard. Tangle Thread never would own she did wrong. She always disputed about it, and was angry when told of her faults. Silver Thread has faults, and often is impatient and angry, and likes to have her own way. But she is sorry when she does wrong, and often tells me so, with tears. Above all, my little Silver

Thread really loves Jesus, and prays to Him to make her like Himself, and He will."

Silver Thread's little thin hand crept softly into her mother's, and her face grew less sorrowful. "It makes me love Jesus to hear mamma talk as if I loved Him," she said to herself. "I believe I do love Him. I am sorry I have been in such a passion. Oh! I wish I hadn't! I wish I hadn't!"

I shall not tell you anything more now about Tangle Thread and Golden Thread.

But I want, before I bid you good-bye, to ask you a question. Are you the little thread in your mother's life that spoils it, or are you the little thread that makes it bright and beautiful? Perhaps you say: "I am not so good as Golden Thread, but I am not half so bad as Tangle Thread." And I dare say you are right. Little children are not often exactly like these. But on the whole, which are you most like? You don't know. Then I beg you to watch yourself one day, and see. And if you find that you are really trying to be good, that you are sorry, and say that you are sorry, when you do wrong; if you sometimes climb into your mamma's lap, and kiss her, and promise to do all you can to please her, then you may safely say to yourself: "I am my dear mother's little Silver or her little Golden Thread. I love her and she loves me, and she wouldn't give me away or sell me for all the treasures in the world."

But if you find that you like to have your own way a great deal better than you like your mamma to have hers; if you pout and cry when you cannot do as you please; if you never own that you are in the wrong, and are sorry for it; never, in short, try with all your might to be docile and gentle, then your name is Tangle Thread, Tangle Thread, and you may depend you cost your mamma many sorrowful hours and many tears. And the best thing you can do, is to go away by yourself and pray to Jesus to make you see how naughty you are, and to make you humble and sorry. Then the old and soiled thread that can be seen in your mother's life will disappear, and, in its place, there will come first a silver, and by-and-by, with time and patience, and God's loving help, a sparkling and beautiful golden one. And do you know of anything in this world you should rather be than somebody's Golden Thread? Especially the Golden Thread of your dear mamma, who has loved you so many years, who has prayed for you so many times, and who longs so to see you gentle and docile, like Him of whom it was said: "Behold the *Lamb* of God!"

LONDON: PRINTED BY EDMUND EVANS, RAQUET COURT, FLEET STREET.

9 781147 828375